Getting Control
of Your Life

GETTING CONTROL OF YOUR LIFE

Rick Yohn

THOMAS NELSON PUBLISHERS
Nashville   Camden   New York

Third printing

Published in Nashville, Tennessee, by Thomas Nelson, Inc. and distributed in Canada by Lawson Falle, Ltd., Cambridge, Ontario.

Printed in the United States of America.

Library of Congress Cataloging in Publication Data

Yohn, Rick.
  How to overcome temptation.

  1. Temptation.   I. Title.
BT725.Y63   248'.4   78–3672
ISBN 0-8407-5836-7

To Rick and Steve, the two great loves of their parents' hearts and God's choice gifts who make parenting a beautiful experience.

To you I dedicate this book, trusting that it will become part of your spiritual heritage to overcome the temptations of life.

"I have no greater joy than this, to hear of my children walking in the truth" (3 John 4).

Contents

Getting Control
of Your Life

1

Born to Win

Do you ever feel like a born loser when you try to fight temptation? Your opponent in this battle begins by hitting you in your most vulnerable spot. As you start to reel, he manages a swift uppercut to the jaw and in a split second your face slams into the floor. "One . . . two . . . three. . . ."

At the count of eight, you stagger to your feet and promise yourself, "That will never happen again. I'll be ready the next time." But the enticement to sin is more powerful than you had anticipated. The enemy promises that what he is offering you is not *really* wrong; he assures you that it is your only way to recognition, love, security, or fulfillment. And so, in a moment of weakness you lower your guard once again. Your opponent's powerful arm crashes through your defense and smashes you to the floor. You lie there in shame with a low self-image and a staggering sense of guilt.

Must we always give in to temptation? Should we just throw in the towel and conclude, "No one is perfect. God never expected me to overcome temptation anyway?" Absolutely not. You were not born to live the rest of your life as a victim of temptation. On the contrary, *you were born to win*.

"But the temptations I face are very powerful," you say. "No one realizes what I have to put up with each day." I know how you feel, but you need to understand that the one experience author and reader, pastor and layman, parent and child have in common is temptation (1 Cor. 10:13). You see, our enemy has an unlimited arsenal to use against us, and he cares not whether we are Christian or atheist, Democrat or Republican, black or white, young or old. He wants all of us to live in defeat; he is not just picking on you alone.

Our opponent's strategy is varied and covers every aspect of life. One of his most devastating weapons is immorality, and with it he is subtly altering the attitudes and life-styles of many Christians.

Immorality confronts us in our living rooms through television's soap operas, crime shows, entertainment specials, and situation comedies. Many R-rated movies (which parents prohibit their children from viewing in the theater) vomit their moral filth into the inner sanctum of the home. The experience of men and women living together outside of marriage is discussed openly and matter-of-factly on television talk shows.

But television is not the only valve allowing moral sewage to drain into our lives. You may be facing the problem at the office, where you are constantly barraged by off-color stories, tales of weekend escapades, double-meaning conversations, and open opportunities for extramarital affairs. If you are a traveling man, you may be experiencing overwhelming moral pressures. You have a hectic schedule during the day and go to an empty, lonely hotel room at night. You go to the magazine rack in the hotel lobby for some reading material and are silently but provokingly solicited by *Playboy* and its companion magazines.

Your teen-age children face similar pressures. Much of the teen's life is wrapped up in music. His idol is often the rock star whose moral life is about as wholesome as the bubonic plague. If the teen-ager accepts the philosophy, life-style, or advice pressed into those plastic discs he listens to, he has little hope for moral survival.

The enemy also attempts to defeat you through your use of time. The battle of setting priorities is as constant as sunrise. How often have you put off the truly important activities for those that, at the time, seemed so urgent? You would probably give anything to recover those precious moments you could have spent with your children, your wife, or your husband if you had not allowed other things to consume your days.

Another part of the enemy's arsenal is the weapon of financial temptation. We are spending ourselves into seemingly irreversible life-styles of financial bondage. "Buy now and pay later" has become the norm, while the biblical mandate to "owe no man anything" is the exception. Many individuals are unaware that God has provided in Scripture many practical, down-to-earth principles for handling money successfully.

The enemy often turns your physical needs for food and water into lustful desires. And to make it easier for your opponent, the church has virtually ignored the problem. Consider, for instance, the subject of overeating. How often have you heard a message on obesity? Most ministers fear to tread on this crate of eggs because Oliver

Overweight is the head deacon. And everyone in the church knows that his wife Hefty Hilda gets all of her clothes tailor made at Tomar's Tents and Awnings! Furthermore, when the minister himself looks like the Gospel Blimp, it is no wonder the subject of overeating is tragically neglected.

Another type of physical temptation dramatically infiltrating the church is the drinking of alcoholic beverages. Christians were formerly encouraged to drink by their working associates, but now the pressure often comes from "nonlegalistic" Christian friends.

These moral, financial, and physical temptations are a mere preview of what you and I can expect from the enemy. He spares no one. Your opponent has been in training for many years. He knows your weaknesses, perhaps better than you know them yourself. It may seem as if you are faced with insurmountable odds. However, you have a lot more going for you than you might expect.

How can a person remain morally pure when he is almost constantly exposed to immoral standards and values? Does the Bible provide practical answers to such pressing issues? You bet it does! Moral temptation is powerful, but God has provided a way for you to be victorious.

Must you succumb to the time trap? No. There *are* ways to manage your time better. The answer is not a twenty-five hour day. Rather, you need to learn what God wants you to do with the time He has already given you.

Is money simply a necessary evil? Wrong again. Has it ever occurred to you that God wants you to enjoy your money? Did you know that He wants you to experience freedom from living hand to mouth? Are you aware that He does not want you to be burdened by a ton of bills every month? You can overcome financial temptations if you are willing to submit your spending habits to biblical principles.

Although at times you may feel like a born loser when battling temptation, always remember: you were born to win. In the following chapters you will discover why temptation makes such an impact when it releases its demonic energy against you. And as you discover the practical biblical principles necessary to combat the enemy, it is my hope you will take courage and strike the deathblow to the common temptations we all consistently encounter.

2

The Devil Made Me Do It

No one knows exactly when the battle between good and evil began. It started somewhere in eternity past, before the creation of man.

Various religions speak about the battle of the gods. Many people today refer to the struggle between two moral forces. But the Scriptures pinpoint the warfare as a battle between God and Satan.

The prophet Isaiah describes Satan prior to his rebellion against God:

How you have fallen from heaven,
O star of the morning, son of the dawn!
You have been cut down to the earth,
You who have weakened the nations!
But you said in your heart,
"*I will* ascend to heaven;
I will raise my throne above the stars of God,
And *I will* sit on the mount of assembly
In the recesses of the north.
I will ascend above the heights of the clouds;
I will make myself like the Most High" (Isa. 14:12-14, italics mine).

Ezekiel further describes Satan's former glory:

You had the seal of perfection, full of wisdom and perfect in beauty. You were in Eden, the garden of God; Every precious stone was your covering. . . . On the day that you were created, they were prepared. You were the anointed cherub. . . . You were blameless in your ways from the day you were created, until unrighteousness was found in you. . . . Your heart was lifted up because of your beauty . . ." (Ezek. 28:12-17).

This being who rebelled against God was part of God's own creation. He was an angel of great beauty and strength. Even the archangel Michael has no personal authority over him (see Jude 9). At one time, he had access to all of heaven and earth, including the Garden of Eden. And it was in that garden that a young woman ran into him unexpectedly, and painfully discovered that he is the primary source of all temptation (see Gen. 3:1-7). From that point on people have been both directly and indirectly challenged by Satan.

In addition to Eve, others in the Bible who have been attacked by Satan himself include Job (see Job 1,2), Jesus (see Luke 4:1-12), Peter (see Matt. 16:23), Judas (see Luke 22:3), and Ananias and Sapphira (see Acts 5:1-11). But since the devil can be only one place at a time, he often confronts us indirectly through other agents.

THE DEVIL'S AGENTS

Satan uses three major allies to help him accomplish his devilish objectives: (1) demons, (2) the world system, and (3) the sinful nature of man. These agents may work you over singly or collectively. Consider first the demonic world.

The Devil's Demons

Demons are those angels who rebelled with Satan in the beginning. The Book of Revelation describes a future battle between the good and evil angelic beings:

And there was war in heaven, Michael and his angels waging war with the dragon. And the dragon and his angels waged war, and they were not strong enough, and there was no longer a place found for them in heaven. And the great dragon was thrown down, the serpent of old who is called the Devil and Satan, who deceives the whole world; he was thrown down to the earth, and his angels were thrown down with him (Rev. 12:7-9).

When the apostle Paul was afflicted by a "thorn in the flesh," he ascribed the source of his trouble to "a messenger of Satan" (2 Cor. 12:7). Demonic activity was so prominent in Jesus' day that part of His ministry included exorcising demons (see Matt. 8:28-34; 12:22). And today, much of our own spiritual warfare is against demonic agents. The Ephesian Christians read these words from Paul, which describe the demonic forces at large in the world:

Finally, be strong in the Lord and in his mighty power. Put on the full armor of God so that you can take your stand against the devil's schemes. For our struggle is not against flesh and blood, but against the *rulers*, against the *authorities*, against the *powers of this dark world* and against the *spiritual forces of evil* in the heavenly realms (Eph. 6:10-12, NIV, italics mine).

The Devil's World

A second agent through which the devil operates is the world system. "We know that we are children of God, and that the whole world is under the control of the evil one" (1 John 5:19, NIV). Jesus referred to the devil as "the ruler of this world" (John 12:31). Paul called him "the god of this world" (2 Cor. 4:4) and "the prince of the power of the air" (Eph. 2:2).

The world system promotes a mind-set opposed to God and His will (see John 7:7; 15:18). It encourages an attitude and philosophy of life that may range anywhere from "there is no God" to "though God exists, I can get along in life without Him."

But how does the devil use this world to influence you for evil? He does so very craftily, through the use of three powerful forces—(1) your own sinful cravings, (2) the lust of your eyes, and (3) your pride in yourself and your possessions. "For everything in the world [i.e., these three forces] comes not from the Father but from the world" (1 John 2:16, NIV).

Sinful Cravings

When God created you, He gave you many natural appetites. The desire for food is one of them. But sometimes that necessary physical desire becomes the means through which Satan tempts you to *crave* or *lust* after food.

Eve allowed her natural desire for food to boil over when she saw that the forbidden tree was "good for food" (Gen. 3:6). After forty days without food, Jesus was told to turn stones into bread (see Luke 4:3). Satan tries to use legitimate physical need to inspire sin.

Another fleshly lust is uncontrolled sexual desire. God built sexual needs into your body. Therefore, you should never feel embarrassed or guilty if you get warm, romantic feelings about someone of the opposite sex. However, those desires must be controlled. Jesus said, "You have heard it said, 'you shall not commit adultery,' but I say to you, that every one who looks on a woman *to lust for her* has committed adultery with her already in his heart" (Matt. 5:27,28, italics mine).

Desires for food and sexual fulfillment are natural and good. But when you gratify those desires outside of God's will, they become lusts of the flesh.

The Lust of the Eyes

Beauty is another attraction that can bring us good or ill. The forbidden fruit was a delight to the eyes. Eve gazed at that fruit until she just had to have it. She allowed its beauty to overpower her.

The Old Testament gives us at least two other examples of how a person can allow what he sees to lead him to sin. One incident involves a soldier who brought God's chastisement upon Israel because he yielded to his lust and disobeyed God's commandment for Israel regarding the spoil of its defeated enemies.

So Achan answered Joshua and said, "Truly I have sinned against the Lord, the God of Israel, and this is what I did; *when I saw* among the spoil *a beautiful mantle* from Shinar and two hundred shekels of silver and a bar of gold fifty shekels in weight, *then I coveted* them and took them; and behold, they are concealed in the earth inside my tent with the silver underneath it" (Josh. 7:20,21, italics mine).

In 2 Samuel 11:2 we read that when David looked upon Bathsheba as she bathed, he saw that she was "very beautiful in appearance." He felt he had to have her for himself or he would never be satisfied. His lust for the beautiful superseded his love for God.

Jesus was confronted with the same kinds of beauty we are. But He was able to resist the temptations to possess what His eyes beheld by looking beyond the outward beauty and focusing on the Creator of all that is beautiful. When Satan showed Jesus all the kingdoms of the world in a moment of time (Luke 4:5), He must have seen much that was truly beautiful. But as Jesus looked on the beauty of those kingdoms, He refused to lust after them.

Beauty is a good quality. We should enjoy the beauty of God's creation, the beauty of a woman and the beauty of the craftsman's handiwork. But when desire for what we see rages uncontrolled and in conflict with God's will for us, it becomes lust.

The Pride of Life

Pride is the other appeal used by the world. It is the attitude of self-sufficiency, expressed in statements such as, "I don't need any help. I can do it myself." Or, "I just ask God to guide me in the big decisions and problems of life. I can handle the rest by myself."

Moses warned his people against pride as they prepared for prosperity:

For the Lord your God is bringing you into a good land of brooks, pools, gushing springs, valleys, and hills; it is a land of wheat and barley, of grape vines, fig trees, pomegranates, olives, and honey; it is a land where food is plentiful, and nothing is lacking; it is a land where iron is as common as stone, and copper is abundant in the hills. When you have eaten your fill, *bless the Lord your God for the good land he has given you.* But that is the time to be careful! Beware that in your plenty you don't forget the Lord your God and begin to disobey him. For when you become full and prosperous and have built fine homes to live in, and when your flocks and herds have become very large, and your silver and gold have multiplied, *that is the time to watch out that you don't become proud, and forget the Lord your God* who brought you out of slavery in the land of Egypt (Deut. 8:7-14, TLB, italics mine).

When Eve saw that the fruit of the tree was "desirable to make one wise" (Gen. 3:6), she wanted to eat the fruit to satisfy her intellect and to be able to boast of knowing all that God knows. And when Satan wanted Jesus to cast Himself off the pinnacle of the temple, he was trying to get Jesus to prove that He was God (Luke 4:9-12).

The world constantly appeals to the ego by feeding us lines such as, "Be a real man by drinking the right kind of beer and smoking the right brand of cigarettes." "Women, you will be swept off your feet by the right man if you choose the right deodorant, use a certain shampoo, and brush your teeth with a toothpaste that gives you sex appeal."

The pride of life has kept many potential believers from the kingdom of God. They find it impossible to admit, "I need Jesus in my life. Without Him, I will find neither salvation nor a purposeful life." The world keeps telling them, "You can do it by yourself. Do your own thing! Be yourself! Don't make a fool of yourself by bowing before God."

The Devil and Your Inner Self

Several years ago a Pogo cartoon appeared that accurately described human nature. Two characters came running up to Pogo shouting, "We've found the enemy. And they is us!" Did anyone ever tell you that you were your own worst enemy? It didn't seem very complimentary, did it? Unfortunately, however, the evidence often overwhelmingly supports that accusation.

At birth you and I inherited the capacity to offend God. The theologians refer to it as the Adamic nature—that natural tendency to sin, compliments of Adam. "When Adam sinned, sin entered the entire human race" (Rom. 5:12, TLB).

James focused on this source of temptation when he wrote, "Let no one say when he is tempted, 'I am being tempted by God'; for God cannot be tempted by evil, and He Himself does not tempt any one. But each one is tempted when he is *carried away and enticed by his own lust*" (James 1:13,14, italics mine).

Paul put it just as graphically when he confessed, "I know I am rotten through and through so far as my old sinful nature is concerned. No matter which way I turn I can't make myself do right. I want to but I can't. . . . So you see how it is: my new life tells me to do right, but *the old nature* that is still inside me loves to sin" (Rom. 7:18,25, TLB, italics mine).

But what does the devil have to do with your inner nature? Quite a lot. Paul traced the root of your sin to Adam (see Rom. 5:12). And since Adam sinned at Satan's suggestion, it is more than likely that he attacks you in a similar fashion.

Satan also affects man's inner nature through a father-child relationship. Jesus declared that man is under one of two fatherhoods—God's or Satan's. He told the Jews, "If God were your Father, you would love Me . . . . You are of your father the devil, and you want to do the desires of your father" (John 8:42,44).

The person who has God as his father possesses a new nature (see 2 Cor. 5:17) as well as the old nature (see Eph. 4:22). But the individual who does not belong to God has only one nature which consistently yields to sin. The Book

of Romans describes the believer's battle between the old
and the new:

So now we can obey God's laws if we follow after the Holy Spirit and
no longer obey the *old evil nature* within us. Those who let themselves
be controlled by their *lower natures* live only to please themselves, but
those who follow after the Holy Spirit find themselves doing those
things that please God. Following after the Holy Spirit leads to life and
peace, but following after the *old nature* leads to death, because the *old
sinful nature* within us is against God. It never did obey God's laws and
it never will. That's why those who are still under the control of their
old sinful selves, bent on following their old evil desires, can never
please God. But you are not like that. You are controlled by your *new
nature* if you have the Spirit of God living in you. (And remember that
if anyone doesn't have the Spirit of Chirst living in him, he is not a
Christian at all)" (Rom. 8:4–9, TLB, italics mine).

THE DEVIL'S STRATEGY

The Holy Scriptures make it clear that our adversary
Satan is no dumbbell. We are not playing war games with
an incredibly naive enemy. The devil is intelligent,
capable of "schemes" (Eph. 6:11), and not easy to figure
out or counterattack. In fact, apart from the Lord we
would have no hope of victory in our war with the god of
this world.

But none of us who enjoy a personal relationship with
Jesus Christ are apart from the Lord. We live in Him and
in Him we can triumph over the forces of evil. But we
must be aware of Satan's strategy, lest we be caught off
guard.

Satan is delighted when he or his demons can help us
doubt the genuineness of God's concern for us. Here is an
example of how he does this:

Now the serpent was more crafty than any beast of the field which the Lord God had made. And he said to the woman, "Indeed, has God said, 'You shall not eat from any tree of the garden'?" And the woman said to the serpent, "From the fruit of the trees of the garden we may eat; but from the fruit of the tree which is in the middle of the garden, God has said, 'You shall not eat from it or touch it, lest you die' " (Gen. 3:1-3).

Without voicing the question for her, man's worst enemy encouraged Eve to ask herself why the one tree was prohibited. Wasn't God being just a bit restrictive and unfair? (Restrictive, yes; unfair, no!)

The devil also seeks to *distort God's Truth*. He is an expert at mixing truth with falsehood. "And the Serpent said to the woman, 'You surely shall not die! For God knows that in the day you eat from it your eyes will be opened, and you will be like God, knowing good and evil" (Gen. 3:4,5). Sure, Adam and Eve learned about good and evil when they obeyed Satan, but there were two facts Satan deliberately lied about or concealed: (1) he said they would not die; and (2) although they could now *see* good and evil, they were also now the devil's slaves *to do* evil.

Of course, the devil's greatest objective is to persuade men to *disobey God*, and one means to this end is to *suggest evil we can do*, as he did with David and later, to no avail, with Jesus.

Then Satan stood up against Israel and moved David to number Israel (1 Chron. 21:1).
Then Jesus was led up by the Spirit into the wilderness to be tempted by the devil (Matt. 4:1).

Satan "does not stand in the truth, because there is no truth in him. Whenever he speaks a lie, he speaks from his own nature; for he is a liar, and the father of lies" (John 8:44). If he can *trick us into believing his deceptions*, he can easily lead us along any path he wants us to follow. "You surely shall not die," the Serpent confidently told Eve (Gen. 3:4). She gullibly agreed and death has been the experience of every human since, including the sinless Son of God.

Eve's experience is a warning to us to be aware of Satan's tactics. Jesus told his disciples to be as "shrewd as serpents, and innocent as doves" (Matt. 10:16). And the apostle John said "Beloved, do not believe every spirit, but test the spirits to see whether they are from God; because many false prophets have gone out into the world" (1 John 4:1).

The devil is a master of *confusion*. The Bible says that ". . . the god of this world has blinded the minds of the unbelieving, that they might not see the light of the gospel of the glory of Christ . . ." (2 Cor. 4:4). Sadly, even those Christians who live selfishly rather than in the power of the Spirit walk in darkness. Therefore, we are admonished to "walk in the light as He Himself is in the light" (1 John 1:7).

Knowing that God wants us to experience His peace at all times, Satan wants to create the opposite within us—he wants us to *live in fear*. "Now the Spirit of the Lord departed from Saul, and an evil spirit from the Lord [here we see God's permissive will in action] terrorized him" (1 Sam. 16:14). The Hebrew word translated "terrorized" means "to terrify or make afraid." Our archenemy wants us to cower in terror. But as believers in Christ, we belong to the one true God, the One who is above all and the One to whom all (including Satan) are accountable and who Himself is accountable to no one. How ridiculous it would be for us to fear Satan's attempts to thwart God's purposes for us.

Satan's desire for us to live in fear is proof that while God is love, Satan is hatred. The same passage that tells us that God is love also says, "Perfect love casts out fear" (1 John 4:18). The devil has no genuine concern for the needs of anyone. In fact, "your adversary, the devil, prowls about like a roaring lion, seeking someone *to devour*" (1 Pet. 5:8, italics mine). But we are eternally God's children—certainly Satan cannot "devour" us! It is true that he cannot transfer anyone from the kingdom of heaven to the kingdom of hell; but he may be able to destroy our peace of mind, our marriage, our testimony, our self-control, or our morality. What can we do? "Be of sober spirit, be on the alert," that same verse tells us. We are also commanded to "walk by the Spirit, and you will not carry out the desire of the flesh" (Gal. 5:16).

Another satanic device is that of afflicting men with *physical and mental infirmities*. Christ personally dealt with demons who caused dumbness (see Luke 11:14), deafness (see Mark 9:25), blindness (see Matt. 12:22), epilepsy (see Mark 1:25,26), and insanity (see Mark 5:1–15). Perhaps not all such problems are produced by demons, but the Scriptures indicate that some are. The challenge to us as the people of God is to praise and trust God throughout all afflictions. Such trust sounds the death knell for Satan's "best" intentions for us.

Lucifer and his armies also specialize in *creating conflict between people*. He especially delights in causing division within the Christian family. Paul had to deal with divisive forces at work in the Corinthian church. In his first letter to the believers there, he spoke of quarrels among them, and explained saying, "Now I mean this, that each one of you is saying, 'I am of Paul,' and 'I of Apollos,' and 'I of Cephas,' and 'I of Christ' " (1 Cor. 1:12). This kind of conflict still goes on, with contemporary variations, and to our shame we are often found cooperating with the devil.

The devil's primary desire today is no different than it was when he first sinned against the God who made him! *Satan wants to be magnified and exalted.* He wants to be Number One; he wants to be God. "I will ascend to heaven; I will raise my throne above the stars of God. . . . I will make myself like the Most High" (Isa. 14:13,14). "Your heart was lifted up because of your beauty," God told his adversary (Ezek. 28:17).

Again, we see the choice we all must make—we must either glorify God or Satan. We must either be free to serve God or be slaves of the worst tyrant of all time for eternity. We can either experience the joy of the Lord or the despair of the devil.

People have asked me, "If God removed Satan from the world, would man still sin?" There is no doubt in my mind that man would continue to sin in spite of the devil's absence. You see, Satan afflicted man with a disease back in the Garden of Eden. And that disease has spread from one generation to another. So even if Satan were removed, the germ (sin) would remain.

When you receive Jesus Christ as your personal Savior, you are not totally cured of that disease. But you are provided with antibodies that will stabilize the disease and keep it from spreading. And the more you yield to the antibodies (new nature), the greater immunity you will build.

Should Satan then be blamed for the sins we commit? Are we right to say, "The devil made me do it"? The answer to both questions is no. Satan cannot *make* us sin. He only has authority to entice us. When we respond to that enticement voluntarily, then we commit sin.

Temptation is Satan's offer to enjoy the temporary pleasures of sin instead of the eternal pleasures of serving God. The devil brings us an offer we wrongly think we cannot refuse. He may entice us with opportunities to perform the "big" sins (adultery, murder, drunkenness), but most of the time he attacks us in areas of our lives we think are safe and under control. We rarely consider how we eat or spend our money or love others or use our tongues or manage our time. Therefore Satan hits us in those areas of our lives we leave uncommitted to God.

Temptation is powerful. And Satan shows mercy to no one. But you need not feel discouraged. In spite of the devil's great power and crafty schemes, you can overcome temptation.

3

I Ate the Whole Thing

Food is one of Satan's most subtle and effective tools for temptation. I personally confess that my Achilles' heel is not located on my foot, but in my stomach.

Satan defeated Adam and Eve through their stomachs. "When the woman saw that the tree was good for food, and that it was a delight to the eyes, and that the tree was desirable to make one wise, she took from its fruit and ate; and she gave also to her husband with her, and he ate" (Gen. 3:6).

The devil tried to defeat Jesus Christ by a similar approach. After the Lord had gone without food for forty days, the tempter challenged him saying, "If you are the Son of God, tell this stone to become bread" (Luke 4:3).

Satan failed to defeat Jesus. But today he is overwhelmingly successful in fattening sheep for slaughter. One out of every three Americans is overweight, and one out of two dies of cardiovascular disease, which is frequently a result of overeating.

It's amazing how blind Christians have become to

Satan's tactics! For years we have preached against the use of alcohol and tobacco, citing health dangers as our primary reasons for advocating abstinence. But as we continue to gorge ourselves, we are neglecting to say anything about the killer habit that affects the majority of us—overeating.

America is a nation of fat people. We are eating ourselves to death. Americans not only eat too much, but we eat the wrong foods as well. Your own "battle of the bulge" may be the result of poor eating habits, emotional problems, or just a lack of discipline. But regardless of the reason, you and I need to change our ways.

THE BIG REFRIGERATOR IN THE SKY

To those who name eating as one of their favorite activities, heaven must be envisioned as a big refrigerator in the sky. And as for their favorite activity—known not so favoritely as gluttony—it is one of the quickest ways of getting to that refrigerator. But, you say, is overeating really that harmful? Judge for yourself.

For some people, overeating causes *heart disease*. Dr. Jean Mayer, Harvard nutrition expert, states, "Heart disease is a problem of an unhealthy life-style, a lack of exercise, and a diet high in fat and salt." Someone else described overeating as "digging your own grave with your teeth," and the Metropolitan Life Insurance Company has found that for every inch your waist exceeds your chest measurement, you can subtract two years off your life. Overeating can also cause high blood pressure, diabetes, and an overall sluggish feeling.

In addition to these physical manifestations, overeating

and its results produce a poor self-image and a lack of discipline in other areas of life (e.g. spending time with the Lord, study habits, keeping the house clean, or other productive activity).

"All right, hold it!" you say. You feel convicted already. Maybe you haven't been watching your intake as you should. Perhaps you are a little on the hefty side. You have tried many times to control your appetite, but nothing has worked. You may be wondering what I can suggest that you haven't already heard of, tried, and failed with.

Listen, I am a fellow sufferer. I have had my share of successes and defeats. And although I cannot offer a lucky rabbit's foot to rub over the bulges and make them disappear, I can share some concrete biblical principles for appetite control. But keep in mind—the principles will be effective only to the degree that you apply them.

OVEREATING IS A SIN

You must be kidding! I mean, let's not get fanatical about the subject. I realize that overeating is a bad habit. But sinful? No way!

Well, let's look at the facts. I believe you would agree that sin is falling short of God's standards, a violation of God's principles. Does overeating fall short of God's standards or violate any of His principles? I believe it does.

Overeating violates the *principle of moderation*, which is one of the primary principles revealed throughout Scripture. Remember when God provided food for Israel in the wilderness? How much did He provide each day? The Scriptures say "a day's portion" (Exod. 16:4). And

He told the people to gather only what they needed, not all that they desired. "Gather of it every man *as much as he should eat*" (Exod. 16:16,18,21, italics mine).

However, there was one incident during the wilderness journey when the moderation principle was violated. The Israelites complained that God wasn't treating them fairly. They were getting tired of manna. They remembered the rich, tasty, fattening foods they used to eat in Egypt. No longer did they want either the amount or the type of food God was faithfully providing. They craved to eat what they wanted and as much as they wanted. God complied with their grumblings in order to teach them a lesson about faith.

"And say to the people, 'Consecrate yourselves for tomorrow and you shall eat meat. . . . You shall eat, not one day, nor two days, nor five days, nor ten days, nor twenty days, but a whole month, until it comes out of your nostrils and becomes loathsome to you; because you have rejected the Lord who is among you and have wept before Him, saying, "Why did we ever leave Egypt?" ' " . . . And the people spent all day and all night and all the next day, and gathered the quail (he who gathered least gathered ten homers*) and they spread them out for themselves around the camp. While the meat was still between their teeth, before it was chewed, the anger of the Lord was kindled against the people, and the Lord struck the people with a very severe plague (Num. 11:18-20, 32,33).

God does not take overindulgence lightly. And He makes no distinction between the overconsumption of food and the overconsumption of alcohol.

Do not be with heavy drinkers of wine [and all God's people said, "Amen. Preach it, brother"],

*One homer – eleven bushels.

Or with gluttonous eaters of meat [and all God's people replied,
"What'd he say? Who does he think he is? Now he's meddling. Let's
change the subject"];
  For the heavy drinker and the glutton will come to poverty,
  And drowsiness will clothe a man with rags (Prov. 23:20,21).

In God's sight there is little difference between the
alcoholic and the "foodaholic."

But do we really eat too much? Am I coming down too
hard on the average American? Friend, I'm just quoting
the facts. Do you realize that you probably eat one
hundred pounds of sugar per year, equaling 174,000
calories? If you are wondering where your "spare tire"
came from, you need not wonder any longer.

But how much food should one consume? There are a
number of considerations that enter into that decision, and
your doctor would best be able to give you personal
guidelines. However, a suggested measurement for
calorie intake is fifteen calories per pound per day. If you
weigh 150 pounds, your daily intake should be 150 x 15 or
2,250 calories per day. If you wish to lose weight, you
must take in less than that amount.

Overeating is sinful because it violates God's principle
of moderation, but the problem does not stop there.
Overeating also violates the *principle of doing that which
is profitable*.

God gave the children of Israel dietary laws so they
would eat foods most profitable for their health. And
when Paul spoke of doing what was profitable, he was
speaking in the context of food. He said, "All things are
lawful for me, but not all things are profitable. All things
are lawful for me, but I will not be mastered by anything.
Food is for the stomach, and the stomach is for food; but

God will do away with both of them . . ." (1 Cor. 6:12,13).

Does food control you or do you control food? Are you eating what is profitable for your health, your self-image, and your productivity in life? It may be lawful for you to eat all those sweets and indulge in evening snacks, but it certainly is not profitable.

Overeating also ignores another of God's principles— *setting a good example for others*. You may be one of those who can eat all you want and still remain slim. This principle is for you in particular. I am not only writing about being overweight; the subject at hand is overeating. When I overeat I gain weight, but you may burn up your extra calories and consequently your sin is not as obvious.

You may ask, "What sin have I committed if I don't gain weight and hurt my health?" Have you ever realized the bad example you may be setting for those of us who gain weight easily? Let's say you take me to a restaurant and tell me to order whatever I want. Following the delicious and slightly fattening main course, you order dessert. Neither of us really needs it, but the choices are very appealing and I decide that since you are paying the bill anyway, I might as well go ahead. You eat dessert and nothing happens. I eat dessert and "shazzam!"—instant flab.

Recently I have come to realize that I have been encouraging my family to overeat by my example. Since I enjoy exercising, I can overeat slightly and then work off the extra calories in a game of racquet ball. But my family does not go in for a lot of exercising, and if they follow my eating habits without exercise, they are in trouble. My overeating sets a very poor example for others.

The words of Paul to the Roman Christians deal with

this cause and effect relationship that our behavior can have on others: "It is good not to eat meat or to drink wine, or to do anything by which your brother stumbles" (Rom. 14:21). We read that Paul practiced what he preached: "Therefore, if food causes my brother to stumble, I will never eat meat again, that I might not cause my brother to stumble" (1 Cor. 8:13).

How do your eating habits affect your friends? Your husband? Your wife? Your children? Your behavior before your children in this area is especially significant. It has been proven that people who were fat as children developed more and larger fat cells than people who were not. This means that if by your example and your words you encourage your children to eat more than they need, you will provide them with a potential problem for life. Parents, watch your eating habits!

Overeating also interferes with *the Spirit's control over our bodies*. You have no doubt heard of the Spirit-controlled life. Have you ever considered the Spirit-controlled body?

God wants to control not only your thoughts, your behavior, and your spending, but also your body. Ask yourself the question, Who is in control of my body when I overeat? The Holy Spirit? If you said yes, try again. This passage from Galatians might help: "But I say, walk by the Spirit, and you will not carry out the desire of the flesh. For the flesh sets its desire against the Spirit, and the spirit against the flesh: for these are in opposition to one another, so that you may not do the things that you please" (5:16,17). Clearly, the fleshly appetite controls you when you eat more than you need.

If you read on in Galatians, you will learn what to expect if you allow God's Spirit to control you. "The fruit of the Spirit is . . . self-control . . ." (5:22,23). God will give us the needed discipline to say no to those extra helpings and to those delicious but destructive snacks. Spirit control and self-control go hand in hand—His hand in ours.

Overeating is sinful because it violates God's principles of (1) moderation, (2) doing what is profitable, (3) setting a good example, and (4) having a Spirit-controlled body. Overeating is not a harmless little indulgence. It is sin. When you have recognized that fact, you will have taken your first step toward conquering the killer habit.

ACCEPT GOD'S WILL FOR YOUR BODY

Did you know that God has a plan for your body as well as for your life? You have already learned that God does not want you to allow food to control your eating habits (see 1 Cor. 6:12,13). Now let's consider three things God does want you to do.

God wants you to *place your body under His control.* "I urge you therefore, brethren, by the mercies of God, to present your bodies a living and holy sacrifice, acceptable to God, which is your spiritual service of worship" (Rom. 12:1). Have you ever presented your body to the Lord? This is not an option; it is a command.

God also wants you to *discipline your body.* Paul compares the Christian's life with an athlete's: "And everyone who competes in the games exercises self-control in all things. . . . Therefore . . . I buffet my body and make it my slave . . ." (1 Cor. 9:25,27).

Paul probably did not jog every day, nor did he work out at the local health spa or YMCA. Rather he exercised and burned up his calorie intake by walking from one place of ministry to another. But you and I are not walkers. We are riders. We ride in the car, the bus, the subway, the commuter train, the elevator, and the escalator. Therefore, we need to make a conscious effort to exercise.

To maintain my proper weight, I must do calisthenics every morning and evening, supplemented throughout the week with racquet ball and jogging. There are many good exercise programs outlined in books. The YMCA, YWCA, health spas, and recreation centers offer physical fitness programs led by those trained in physical education. You must decide what you enjoy and what you can afford. But it is important that you discipline your body with exercise.

Of course, exercise alone is insufficient. You have to learn to say no to certain foods and to too much food. Several years ago I exercised as though I were preparing for the Olympics. I felt great. My weight was right for me and I discovered I could even enjoy ice cream several nights a week without any weight gain. But when my exercise program dwindled, my eating pattern continued. You can guess what happened. So, learn to discipline your body with a good balance of exercise and proper food intake.

Finally, God wants you to *glorify Him in your body*. Paul expressed his greatest objective in life when he wrote, ". . . according to my earnest expectation and hope, that I shall not be put to shame in anything, but that with all boldness, Christ shall even now, as always, *be exalted in my body*, whether by life or by death" (Phil. 1:20, italics mine). When he wrote to the Corinthians he stated, "For you have been bought with a price: therefore *glorify God in your body*" (1 Cor. 6:20, italics mine). You should glorify God in your body because (1) your body is a "member of Christ" (1 Cor. 6:15), (2) your body is "a temple of the Holy Spirit" (1 Cor. 6:19a), and (3) your body does not belong to you, but to the Lord (1 Cor. 6:19b,20).

Pause a moment and answer the following questions:
1. Is it God's will for me to eat the way I do?
2. Is it God's will for me to be overweight?
3. Is it God's will for me to have no control over my intake?
4. Am I glorifying Him in my body by the way I look?

You may feel like giving up now, but don't. Keep reading. Others have found victory over this problem and so can you.

PRACTICAL WAYS TO CURB YOUR APPETITE

Aim for a change in life-style, not just another short-term diet. You have probably tried the low carbohydrate diet, the grapefruit diet, and the high protein diet. Thanks to Dr. Stillman, you drank enough water to need an immediate kidney transplant. But if you are like most dieters, you gained back what you lost within a year after your diet.

You did not gain your weight back because the diet you tried was a poor one—obviously if you lost weight it served its intended purpose. Rather, the problem has to do with a cycle you are no doubt familiar with. First, your overeating causes you to gain weight and feel guilty. And so to relieve the guilt, you go on a crash diet. During the diet, you start to feel like a true martyr. When you have made a significant sacrifice and have lost several pounds, you decide you deserve a reward. You start eating some of the foods you had given up during your diet, and before long you have returned to the same eating habits you had before you started. The only way to break this cycle and maintain your proper weight is to change your day-to-day eating habits.

Eat smaller amounts at a slower pace. You will help your digestive system and also enjoy your food more if you follow this principle. In many cultures, eating is a way of fellowship, but for many Americans it is merely a pit stop consisting of rushing in, filling up, and running out to do something more urgent. But when you eat more slowly, you will not eat as much. Whenever I practice this, I never leave the table feeling gorged.

Give up those night snacks. This is probably the most difficult change to accept. Has your theme song become "I've grown accustomed to those snacks"? I can identify with that.

Ice cream is one of my favorite foods. When I was growing up in Pennsylvania, a typical evening snack was ice cream and pretzels. (I guess you have to be a Pennsylvania Dutchman to appreciate the combination.) My other food waterloo is jelly beans. I love to reach into a candy dish and grab a colorful handful of those mouth watering gems. After giving the black ones to my wife or my dog, I sit back and pop the others in my mouth, sucking them, chewing them, or just letting them melt in my mouth. But my new life-style demands that I refuse to snack on either ice cream or jelly beans at night.

You may feel it is impossible to give up all snacks at night. If that is the case, I suggest you substitute celery or carrots for the sweet stuff. It won't be too long before you can give up the night snacks altogether.

Fight the battle at the grocery store, rather than at home. Once that junk food gets into my house, I have nearly lost the battle. If I don't buy it, I can't eat it. It also helps if I eat before I go to the grocery store. That way I am less tempted to buy more than I need. There is one problem with this plan—I seldom buy the groceries. Sometimes my wife brings home goodies, but I can tell you, once they are in the house, they are devoured. Do yourself a favor—don't buy junk foods. Keep them out of your house. Then when you are invited to eat out, you can enjoy the dessert.

Eat more fruit. Earlier you learned that the average American eats one hundred pounds of sugar each year. On top of all that sugar, you can add other carbohydrates. For instance, sugar is one hundred percent carbohydrate, bread is fifty percent carbohydrate, a banana is twenty-two percent, and an apple is fourteen percent. The result is catastrophic. It makes quite a difference whether you go to bed with a dish of ice cream or an apple in your system.

Refuse to change your clothing size. I am speaking, of course, to those of us who have stopped growing up and have started growing out. When those sides begin to bulge and your circulation slows because of the tightness, accept it as a warning signal. It is time to change your eating habits, not your clothes.

Focus on the rewards of bodily discipline. The Bible indicates that your self-image often determines your behavior: "For as he thinks within himself, so he is" (Prov. 23:7). There is value in seeing yourself as other than being overweight and fighting a continuous problem. Paul wrote, "Finally, brethren, whatever is true, whatever is honorable, whatever is right, whatever is pure, whatever is lovely, whatever is of good repute, if there is any excellence and if anything worthy of praise, let your mind dwell on these things" (Phil. 4:8).

Here is how one person applied this principle and won her own bulge battle:

Visualize yourself at the weight you want or need to be. Then in your prayer life (which should always be expanded, no matter how much you presently pray!), give that image of yourself to God, think of yourself as that person before God, and ask his strength and his willpower to enable you to become that person.

The more you pray, the more weight you will lose. It's difficult to end a session of prayer about losing weight and go to the kitchen to consume a sundae. Not that it can't happen, particularly at first, but you'll tolerate that less and less as you *persist* in praying. And you can thank God that failures won't continue!*

Pause a moment and begin to think of how great it would be to feel better and look trim once again. Think of yourself going into the doctor's office and hearing him say, "You are in great health. Blood pressure is normal, and you have lost all that dangerous excess fat." See yourself doing the things you once enjoyed, but because of your weight you have had to give up. Above all, see yourself standing before the Lord and hearing Him say, "Well done, good and faithful servant. Enter into the rewards of your labor: good health, a better self-image, more energy, and a God-honoring body."

How little can I eat and maintain my health? Most of us have been taught to clean our plates. Remember your mother saying, "Now eat everything on your plate.

*Nance Wabshaw, "I Prayed My Pounds Away," *The Christian Reader*, (Jan./Feb. 1977), p. 78.

People are starving around the world and they would love to have what you don't eat. So don't waste your food." There is excellent advice in such an admonition. We should not waste food, and we should do something for the starving millions. They *would* love to have what many Americans do not eat. However, eating everything on your plate does not necessarily follow in logical sequence.

You can avoid waste by putting less on your plate. Furthermore, you should eat only what you need to eat. True, multitudes die of starvation every day. But people also die of diseases and body stress caused by overeating. Begin to eat only what you need, even if you leave food on your plate. Eventually, you will learn to take smaller portions and finish what you take. Remember to ask yourself, "How much do I need to maintain my health?"

Before we move on to the last two principles, think through what you have already read. How can you best deal with overeating?

(1) Accept the fact that overeating is sinful.

(2) Accept God's will for your body.

(3) Adopt practical ways to curb your appetite.

These principles are valid. If put into practice, they will produce excellent results. However, there are two other exhortations that will help you put everything in gear.

ADMIT THAT YOU HAVE A PROBLEM
WITH OVEREATING

Remember when you first came to know Jesus personally? You had to admit your need for salvation before you received it. Likewise, if you want to experience deliverence from overeating, first admit your problem to God.

When Adam ate the fruit, he refused to accept personal responsibility. He excused his indulgence by blaming "the woman Thou gavest to be with me" (Gen. 3:12). Many husbands are still using a modified version of that excuse.

Today you hear, "But my wife is such a fantastic cook. I just can't turn down what she makes. It would hurt her feelings." This is where husband and wife must have a conference. There is no need to forever give up cooking those goodies. If you wives will cut back on how often you bake pies and cookies, your husbands will be able to eat less and stay trim. This suggestion might also help you, if you are struggling with a weight problem.

Another excuse is, "I eat like a horse because my parents ate that way." I know I have developed some poor eating habits from childhood, but my parents are not forcing me to continue the same eating pattern today.

And finally we might blame "the appetite thou gavest me." True, God gave each of us an appetite for food since birth. But who develops that appetite?

Admitting that a problem exists is the first step in solving it. Here is a suggested prayer that deals with the problem: "Lord, I confess to You that I overeat. I will no longer blame anyone else. I know that I'm hurting my body and dishonoring You. Forgive me for my abuse."

If you have come to the point of truly confessing this sin to God, you are ready for the final step.

GIVE YOUR APPETITE TO GOD

Perhaps you have been willing to give God your finances, your family, and your future. But for some reason you have been reluctant to give your appetite to God. This is the moment of truth. You can continue reading this book as though it were meant for someone else, or you can make a personal commitment to the Lord right now:

Lord, here is my appetite. You know I have not been able to control it. So I give it to you. Give me the controls I need. Teach me to say no to the wrong kinds of food as well as the wrong amounts of food. In Jesus' name, Amen."

It is God's will that you eat properly. So you are guaranteed that He will answer this prayer (see 1 John 5:14,15). Now thank Him for the answer and expect Him to control your appetite.

I have found I must renew my commitment to the Lord each day, usually before I eat or at night when I am tempted to snack. I will continue to follow this pattern until my eating habits take on a significant change.

Don't allow the devil easy access to your appetite. But rather, "Submit therefore to God. Resist the devil and he will flee from you" (James 4:7).

4

To Drink or Not to Drink

What do astronaut Bud Aldrin, movie and TV stars Dana Andrews, Jan Clayton, Garry Moore, Dick Van-Dyke, and Robert Young, former senator Harold Hughes and former congressman Wilbur Mills, singer Greg Mitchell, and athlete Don Newcombe have in common? Each is a self-confessed recovered alcoholic.

At one time, they were nondrinkers. Then each began drinking in moderation. But as the pressures of life increased, their alcohol consumption also increased. Eventually, each of these celebrities lost control of his drinking habit. Like nine million other Americans, they began what seemed an innocent, enjoyable pastime. But within a few years they became enslaved to a destructive, merciless master—alcohol.

Alcoholism is not limited to celebrities. The seeds for ruined lives are being planted in many homes, Christian and non-Christian. In fact, in some evangelical circles social drinking is the latest in-thing.

WHY IS DRINKING SO TEMPTING?

For some, drinking offers no temptation whatsoever. But for many Christians, the problem stares them in the face wherever they turn. Business associates, mass media advertising, and fellow Christians may be subtly pressuring them to join the sophisticated group of drinkers.

Television commercials bombard every living room with the appeal to change from teetotaler to moderate drinker. During the football season, millions of sports fans hear all about the best beers. To some, an athletic event without beer is like a banana split without the banana. The implied question is no longer whether to drink, but what to drink.

Drinking is a temptation to some because if offers them an instant escape from life's pressures. The present generation could be labeled "the chemical generation." If you feel depressed, take a pill and turn on. If you are too uptight, take another pill or a glass of alcohol and unwind. Whatever your mood, you can change it within a few minutes by means of some drug—pills, marijuana, or alcohol.

Others may drink as a way to establish a new self-image. You may want to reflect the image of independence. As a Christian, you perhaps have determined not to associate with legalists who live according to a long list of "thou shalt nots." So you flex that independent spirit and wave the banner for "Christian liberty." You cite 1 Corinthians 9:4 and Matthew 7:1 as your freedom declaration: "Do we not have a right to eat and drink?" and "Do not judge lest you be judged yourselves." (You would do well to read those verses in context.)

A person who drinks alcohol might be trying to project the "tough guy" or "good sport" image. You never see a ninety-pound weakling advertising beer; it is almost always the athletic, good-sport, one-of-the-boys types. The ads imply that the beer drinker does not concern himself with culture. He is more concerned about the nuts and bolts of life and having a good time.

But perhaps this last image doesn't appeal to you. You like a more sophisticated approach to life. You enjoy fine restaurants and want to be seen with the cultured crowd. The wine makers have just the product to give you instant culture and sophistication.

One further reason why alcohol is such a great temptation is its availability. Alcohol is found in most restaurants, grocery stores, airplanes, parties, and homes. The majority of children and teen-agers who decide to "try" drinking usually find a sufficient supply at home.

WHY DO CHRISTIANS DRINK?

Do Christians and non-Christians drink for the same reasons? In many instances they do: to relax, to escape from problems and pressures, to feel part of the group, and for sheer enjoyment.

But because most Christians would not find those reasons sufficient for justifying their drinking before believers who do not drink, other reasons are implemented.

Some Christians may cite drinking as a family tradition that came out of their ethnic or geographical background. I might suggest that such a tradition be guided by the principle of 1 Corinthians 10:12: "Therefore let him who thinks he stands take heed lest he fall." You may reason,

"Moderate drinking never hurt my parents or relatives and it won't hurt me." However, you may be more susceptible to a problem with alcohol because of a physical condition or because of the pressures you daily encounter. The ability of your relatives and friends to handle alcohol provides no guarantee that you or others in your family can handle it.

Another justification for Christians' drinking is the fact that Jesus drank wine. In fact, Jesus said that His enemies called Him 'a gluttonous man and a drunkard'' (Matt. 11:19), not because of any abuse but because of His association with sinners.

Jesus did not drink grape juice; in all probability He did drink wine. But never forget that Jesus had full control over everything He did (see Heb. 4:15). Can you guarantee total control over your intake of alcoholic beverages? Jesus also counseled with prostitutes and remained pure. Do you feel the same confidence in that area of life? Jesus encountered Satan face to face and defeated him. Have you won all of your encounters with the tempter? Yes, Jesus drank wine. But should I expose myself to a potential problem because He could drink without becoming a problem drinker?

Some Christians might suggest that they drink because the apostle Paul encouraged Timothy to drink. Their premise is partially true, but there is more to the story. Timothy experienced a common problem of his day— stomach disorder due largely to the foul drinking water. Today the identical problem exists in many countries. For many people around the world wine, taken in moderation, would be a safer drink than common water.

Paul wrote to Timothy, "No longer drink water

exclusively, but use a little wine for the sake of your stomach and your frequent ailments" (1 Tim. 5:23). Consider the following three observations. First, Paul makes a contrast between drinking water *only* and drinking wine *sometimes*. Second, Paul includes the adjective "little." And finally, the purpose for wine drinking in this context is medicinal. There was no "plop plop, fizz fizz" to relieve stomach problems in those days.

Another argument offered in favor of wine and beer drinking is that the alcohol content is low. However, this argument is like saying that if you eat pastries with fewer calories, you won't have to worry about weight gain. Anything taken in excess causes undesirable consequences.

Remember good old Noah? He was a righteous man. He walked with God. He was faithful in building an ark, and God spared him from perishing in the flood. But soon after the waters subsided, Noah left the ark and planted a vineyard. He apparently had an extremely profitable harvest, and so he made wine from his grapes and began to drink. But Noah celebrated until he got drunk; he was a God-fearing man, but he could not handle his liquor (see Gen. 9:21).

Another righteous man who thought he could handle a small amount of alcohol was Lot. His daughters' plot against him is unveiled in Genesis 19:32: "Come, let us make our father drink wine, and let us lie with him, that we may preserve our family through our father." Lot became so intoxicated he did not remember what happened during the night.

In her autobiography, Norma Zimmer shares her family background with the reader. Her father and mother were both alcoholics. The beverage they most often consumed was wine—the drink with the low alcoholic content of twelve percent.

Probably the least defendable reason some Christians give for drinking is "to resist a drink would be offensive to a host and turn him off to Christianity." To that, Amy Vanderbilt would have replied, "Only a poor host would insist that guests drink."

What would offend a host—the fact that you turned down a drink or the manner in which you turned it down? You can graciously refuse a drink by saying, "No thank you. I appreciate your generosity, but I'd prefer a Coke" (or milk or water). Or you could be obnoxious and reply, "Why are you offering *me* a drink? Don't you know that I'm a *Christian*? Christians don't drink! Alcohol is of the devil! And I don't want *any* of that *sinful* stuff flowing through *my* veins!"

Consider how you treat those who don't drink coffee. Do you get upset and feel that it is a put-down because some refuse coffee? Certainly not. You would never respond by saying, "What are you anyway? Some religious nut? What's wrong with drinking coffee?" One can graciously turn down an alcoholic beverage without offending the host just as one can substitute milk for coffee without fear of offense.

FOUR PRINCIPLES TO CONSIDER
BEFORE DRINKING ALCOHOL

To drink or not to drink is a question you need to answer for yourself. Here are a few principles that may help you frame your convictions.

Consider the Dangers of Alcohol

Alcohol has both potential and actual dangers built into its very nature. What has alcohol already accomplished for Americans? Statistics show there are nine million alcoholics in America today. In a recent five-year period, 125,000 Americans were killed on U. S. highways. Half of these were killed by drunken drivers.

Furthermore, recent statistics revealed that 35,000 persons in one year were jailed for violent crimes committed while someone involved in the crime was under the influence of alcohol.

In addition to the deaths and crimes related to alcohol, one might include the adverse effect this drug has on the human body. Alcohol is a depressant on the brain center and destroys irreplaceable brain cells. It inflames and destroys the cells of the liver, the only bodily organ that can burn alcohol. Alcohol also affects the heart.

These are examples of the actual damage caused by alcohol. But there are also significant potential dangers.

Drinking alcohol, even in moderation, may set a negative precedent for your children and friends. You may maintain complete control of yourself when you drink, but can you guarantee that if beer, wine, or liquor is available in your home, it will be a good influence on your children? Can you be certain that when you are not home your children will not get the idea of "trying it out"? Will your children or friends use these beverages with the same degree of moderation you have displayed? Most parents would never allow marijuana into their homes for fear their children would try it and eventually progress to harder drugs. Why then do many of these same parents think nothing of having beer and wine around the house, unconcerned that their children might develop an appetite for alcohol from less intoxicating spirits and move on to harder liquors? Isn't there an inconsistency here?

Paul emphasizes the danger of setting a bad example for others:

And if your brother is bothered by what you eat, you are not acting in love if you go ahead and eat it. Don't let your eating ruin someone for whom Christ died. Don't do anything that will cause criticism against yourself even though you know that what you do is right. For, after all, the important thing for us as Christians is not what we eat or drink but stirring up goodness and peace and joy from the Holy Spirit. . . . The right thing to do is to quit eating meat (offered to idols) or drinking wine or doing anything else that offends your brother or makes him sin (Rom. 14:15-17, 21, TLB).

A second potential problem is the harm you might do to yourself. Your casual drinking now could lead you to excessive drinking as you face greater pressures in life. The only guaranteed way to prevent any personal problem with alcohol is to abstain.

Another potential danger from alcohol is that it can lead an individual to say or do things he later regrets.

Wine gives false courage; hard liquor leads to brawls; what fools men are to let it master them, making them reel drunkenly down the street! (Prov. 20:1, TLB). Wine, women, and song have robbed my people of their brains (Hos. 4:11, TLB). Whose heart is filled with anguish and sorrow? Who is always fighting and quarreling? Who is the man with bloodshot eyes and many wounds? It is the one who spends long hours in the taverns, trying out new mixtures. Don't let the sparkle and the smooth taste of strong wine deceive you. For in the end it bites like a poisonous serpent; it stings like an adder. You will see hallucinations and have delirium tremens, and you will say foolish, silly things that would embarrass you no end when sober. (Prov. 23:29-33, TLB).

Alcohol is dangerous. Yet danger in itself does not always deter one from taking risks. Statistics overwhelmingly link certain cancers to smoking, but millions of people—including doctors—continue to smoke. Auto safety experts often give evidence of serious injury and fatalities that could have been avoided by using seat belts. Still millions of Americans would rather sit on their seat belts than in them. And so it is with alcohol. Many do not take the dangers seriously.

The Use of Wine by First-Century Christians Is Not a Blank Check for Present-Day Use

First-century life in Palestine has little in common with twentiety-century life in America. Biblical Palestine was primarily an agricultural society. The average citizen maintained his own vineyard or had access to a neighbor's. Wine-making in the home was common.

As mentioned earlier, the drinking water in Palestine and surrounding areas was often impure, causing stomach and intestinal disorders such as dysentery. One way to combat this problem was to add wine to the water; the alcohol purified the water and probably improved the taste.

A verse from one of the books of the Apocrypha, written during the intertestamental period, offers evidence for this practice: "It is harmful to drink wine alone or water alone, whereas mixing wine with water makes a more pleasant drink that increases delight . . ." (2 Macc. 15:39, NAB). Palestine's wine during biblical times probably contained as much alcohol as many present-day medicines.

True, even with such a low level of alcohol, people still became intoxicated, but this was not morally acceptable. So before you conclude, "What was good enough for the apostle Paul is good enough for me," consider the contrasts between then and now.

Do Not Substitute Alcohol for the Holy Spirit

I am becoming more and more convinced that alcohol is the world's substitute for the Holy Spirit. Alcoholic beverages offer the consumer a release of tension, greater sociability, a better self-image, greater strength, peer acceptance, and the determination to face life's problems victoriously.

It is not just a coincidence that Paul warned, "And do not get drunk with wine, for that is dissipation, but be filled with the Spirit" (Eph. 5:18). There are parallels between the two conditions. Both wine and the Holy Spirit can exert a strong influence on the recipient. Also, each is capable of effecting a different life-style. The Holy Spirit can relieve tension, make you more sociable, give you a better self-image, provide you with inner strength, make you attractive to your peers, and help you face life's problems victoriously.

On the other hand, the Holy Spirit has none of the potential dangers inherent in wine. You never need be embarrassed when you speak under the influence of God's Spirit. Nor will you be a nuisance to your family or society. You will have no fears of setting a questionable example for your children, and the Holy Spirit has no ill effects on the human body.

Is it any wonder Paul encouraged his readers to be filled

with the Holy Spirit? Should it be surprising that he would tell believers to walk in the Spirit (see Gal. 5:16)?

Focus on What Is Profitable Rather Than on What Is Lawful

"All things are lawful for me, but not all things are profitable. All things are lawful for me, but I will not be mastered by anything. . . . All things are lawful, but not all things are profitable. All things are lawful, but not all things edify" (1 Cor. 6:12; 10:23).

Wine drinking is lawful for Christians. God will not strike you dead if you drink. But as you think back over this chapter, try to determine if moderate drinking is either profitable or edifying. Evaluate its dangers. Consider the historical, cultural, and social context of biblical wine drinking. Then decide for yourself, "As for me and my house we will/will not drink."

5

The Last of the Big Spenders

Bills. Bills. Bills. You succumbed to the temptation to "buy now and pay later" and "later" is now here. You are getting those nasty impersonal letters saying "pay up or else!" Has indebtedness become a way of life for you?

Or maybe you are one of those few who have not fallen into the instant credit trap. But even so, you may sometimes feel that your finances are in disorder because of your "easy come, easy go" mentality. Do you find yourself wondering where in the world your money has gone?

A few years ago, I began to realize that my family and I lacked financial freedom because of our undisciplined use of money. Haggai's warning echoed through my head: "You plant much but harvest little. You have scarcely enough to eat or drink, and not enough clothes to keep you warm. Your income disappears, as though you were putting it into pockets filled with holes!" (Hag. 1:6, TLB). The pieces of the puzzle were beginning to fit.

Since I couldn't pay our bills on time, I was paying a

high interest note each month. I worried about financial commitments, even though the Lord told me, "Don't worry about things—food, drink, and clothes. For you already have life and a body—and they are far more important than what to eat and wear" (Matt. 6:25, TLB). At times I would catch myself feeling covetous toward those who possessed what I could not afford (see Ps. 73:2,3). I concluded that my basic problem was *financial bondage*.

But I did not want to accept all the responsibility for my financial problems; and so I searched for a scapegoat—my wife and her check-writing procedure fit that role nicely. When a bill didn't get paid on time, I blamed her. I was expecting her to play God and create something out of nothing.

In addition to the family tension I was causing by blaming my wife for our financial difficulties, I began to feel *I was robbing God* (Mal. 3:7-12). Although my wife and I were tithing our income, we often delayed our giving to make other payments. Furthermore, we wanted to give more, but always the question, "How can we afford to give any more to the Lord's work when we aren't paying our bills on time?" kept us from increasing our tithe.

Because of these pressures, my spiritual life hit a plateau. With so much energy consumed in frustration over money matters, I had little energy left to focus on the Lord (see Mark 4:19). And if I as a pastor did not have my financial head screwed on properly, how could I be of help to others facing similar problems?

These experiences of financial bondage and the resulting guilt and spiritual dryness were eroding my peace of mind. But I soon realized that none of these circumstances was the real issue. Each was only a symptom of the deeper problem—overspending. And I was the culprit. So I decided on a plan of action that eventually helped me resist the temptation of overspending.

HOW TO KICK THE HABIT OF OVERSPENDING

Overspending From God's Viewpoint

One way to find temporary relief from guilt caused by overspending is to compare your financial mismangement with someone who has a chronic case of the same disease. But eventually you ought to see yourself from God's perspective, and if you are like me, you won't like what you see.

The Bible calls the poor manager an unfaithful steward (Matt. 25:24–28). You see, the believer is the steward or manager of God's money. And an unfaithful steward is a Christian who mismanages that money by overspending, squandering, hoarding, or refusing to give to the Lord's work.

When Israel mismanaged God's provisions, He called them "robbers" (Mal. 3:8). Jesus referred to money worriers as those who "choke the Word" (Mark 4:19); He thinks of those who hoard money as "fools" (Luke 12:19–21); and those who squander their resources are "unprepared for the Lord's return" (Luke 12:35–48). Not a very pretty picture, is it?

Evaluate Your Present Spending Habits

After realizing I had to face my financial problems in order to solve them, I decided to take the past three months of canceled checks and learn where our money had gone. I was shocked to discover how many installment debts we owed—a charge-all credit card company, several department stores, and the credit union. No wonder we couldn't make ends meet! (I later read that installment debts should not exceed twenty-five percent of your total income. Ugh!) I also noticed that we could cut back on several items such as unnecessary gadgets, eating out, and junk foods (those munchies for night snacks).

Decide Who Is Going to Handle the Finances

Before going any further with my plan, I knew I would have to take over the bill-paying, a responsibility my wife had always handled. And was I in for a surprise! For years I thought my wife wanted to write the checks and keep the books. After all, she was the brains in the family. Math was never my department. When we married, I thought it only made sense for her to handle our finances.

Therefore, when I suggested that I take over the finances I expected a quite different reaction from the one I got. Rather than hard feelings, there were expressions of joy and relief. She replied, "I hated that responsibility. I'm so glad you're taking over."

Shocked? Pleasantly. And with the financial responsibility resting squarely on my shoulders and the help of an inexpensive calculator, I was able to discover ways to regain financial freedom.

Avoid Impulse Buying

I have always liked a good bargain. There was a time when I would buy something at a discount even if I didn't

need it. But now I follow these guidelines:
(1) Don't buy anything on the spur of the moment.
(2) It's not a bargain unless I need it or can use it profitably.
(3) Make certain the discount price is a true discount and not a markdown from an inflated price.
(4) Be certain the merchandise is good quality.
(5) Do comparative shopping first. I may find what I want at a better price elsewhere.

Consistently following these guidelines has proven effective in curbing my impulse buying. A few months ago I was able not only to see how much control I have gained over my spending, but also to demonstrate for my sons ways to resist the temptation of buying impulsively.

My sons and I were at a local shopping center when we stopped to listen to a salesman playing an organ outside a music store. I knew if we stayed long we would be bombarded with a sales pitch. Sure enough, within seconds after we had stopped the salesman greeted me, played up to my boys, and then asked the younger one, "Wouldn't you like your daddy to buy one of these fine organs for you?" Both sons looked at me with hopeful eyes. I asked the price. "Normally it's $2,300. But this weekend only, it's $1,899." I told him I might be interested some time in the future, but not now. But soon we were ushered into a practice room where he taught the boys to play a song. Within a few minutes, each played the song with the full rhythm of drums and other percussion.

Ricky and Steven were really excited. And the price for the very same organ had now dropped to $1,799. Still no deal. A short time later the salesman was on the phone pleading with his boss. Finally he turned to me to make the final offer, "My boss said if you will leave a small down payment to hold this organ, you can have it for $1,699 and we will deliver it tomorrow." This time the boys thought they had hit a gold mine. But I politely turned down the offer. We left the store, leaving behind a dejected salesman. Then I explained to my sons what had actually taken place.

I asked, "Do you think the salesman was interested in us or in his commission?" They agreed that his interest was probably in the commission. I explained that this is the way he makes a living, and that he should try his best to sell his product. However, I also pointed out that when a salesman gets as desperate to sell something as this one did, his interest in the buyer has virtually vanished.

Then I asked the boys if they felt we needed an organ. Both agreed that we could probably do without one for the time being. They also agreed that we had not shopped anywhere else to compare prices. Even though their emotions were still attached to the organ, their logic agreed that it was best to keep the organ at the store.

If I had encountered an incident like this a few years ago, I would have been ripe for the plucking. But by following a few basic guidelines I am no longer the salesman's ideal customer.

Go Back to the Cash System—Especially for Luxuries

This principle also played a part in my decision on the organ. I told my sons that luxury items should be paid for in cash. Even though I had the borrowing power, I would not use borrowed money for unnecessary things. By luxury items I mean those things we would like to have but which are not essential for life, health or job.

This means you may have to wait until you can afford such products. I have wanted a new 35 millimeter camera with a zoom lens for five years. I never have the cash, and so it remains an unfulfilled dream. But one day that luxury item will become a reality. However, it will have to wait until my other priorities are fulfilled.

Plan Your Spending in Light of Biblical Priorities

I want to make certain that whatever else I do about finances, I follow a biblical priority system. Therefore, *God must take first place in my financial management.* Jesus spoke quite often about money matters. On one occasion He said, "But seek first His kingdom and His righteousness; and all these things shall be added to you" (Matt. 6:33). I should not place my wants and debts ahead of the Lord's work. A better priority system would be to give to the Lord's work, pay my bills, and then buy what is needed with what remains.

This often means I cannot buy all those gadgets I would like to have. But it is far better to deny my wants than to tip God with leftovers. He must receive the firstfruits of my paycheck.

The second priority involves *the needs of my family.* The New Testament explains, "But anyone who won't care for his own relatives when they need help, especially those living in his own family, has no right to say he is a Christian. Such a person is worse than the heathen" (1 Tim. 5:8, TLB).

But what are their needs? Jesus lists them in His Sermon on the Mount: "So my counsel is: Don't worry about things—food, drink, and clothes. . . . Your heavenly

Father already knows perfectly well that you need them, and he will give them to you *if you give him first place in your life* and live as he wants you to" (Matt. 6:25,32,33, TLB, italics mine). If I take care of priority number one, God promises to provide priority number two.

The third priority focuses on *the future needs of my family*. I had never before realized that the Bible emphasizes the importance of preparing for future needs. "Take a lesson from the ants, you lazy fellow. Learn from their ways and be wise! For though they have no king to make them work, yet they labor hard all summer, gathering food for the winter" (Prov. 6:6-8, TLB). The ant is commended for its wisdom in preparing for future needs, and so is the wise housewife—"She has no fear of winter for her household, for she has made warm clothes for all of them" (Prov. 31:21, TLB).

Furthermore, in the parable of the unfaithful steward, the master rebukes his steward for failing to prepare for the future: "Wicked man! Lazy slave! Since you knew I would demand your profit, you should at least have put my money into the bank so I could have some interest" (Matt. 25:26,27, TLB).

Future needs may include life and health insurance, savings for education, emergency savings, sound investments, and a retirement program. This is not the same thing as hoarding. How much you put aside is your decision, but it should be in keeping with your first two priorities.

The fourth priority is expressed in *my personal wants*. The Bible does not say it is sinful to have wants. Sin enters only when the wants are fulfilled at the expense of other priorities. I still want that camera, but not at the expense of priorities one, two, and three. Furthermore, my family's wants, such as new furniture and other items for the house, take precedence over my own wants.

As you meet those other priorities, you need not feel guilty about buying a few wants. The Bible clearly states that God ". . . richly supplies us with all things to enjoy" (1 Tim. 6:17). Jesus said, "If you then, being evil, know how to give good gifts to your children, how much more shall your Father who is in heaven give what is good to those who ask Him!" (Matt. 7:11).

Do you only give your children gifts they need on Christmas Day? Or do you give them some gifts they don't really need, but would tremendously enjoy? Likewise, your Father in heaven wants to give you enjoyment gifts as well as need gifts. As you honor Him with your finances, He will abundantly bless you with His gifts, in His own time and way.

Caution—never give to get. Give because it is right. Give to express your love for God. Give to meet the needs of others. But as you give, you can be certain that God will bless you.

Remove All Unnecessary Credit Cards

Probably one of the greatest hindrances to financial freedom is the abuse of the credit card. Some people use the credit card like an Aladdin's Lamp. Rub three times and Poof! Instant ownership! But when the Genie goes back into his lamp, Aladdin has to pay those drawn out, high-interest bills.

My wife and I have trimmed our credit cards to one charge-all type (primarily for identification purposes when writing checks) and two from oil companies. We have also made a commitment to pay all debts when due to avoid the interest payment.

Pay Your Present Bills Before You Accumulate More Debt

This principle is probably violated more than the others, and that is why so many get into such great debt.

I used to be especially susceptible to getting further into debt after I had borrowed money to consolidate payments. Soon I would rationalize, "Now that I'm not making so many payments, I can afford to buy a few more wants."

I have come to realize two great fallacies in that attitude. (1) It drives a person into greater financial bondage, and (2) it violates a scriptural command— "Don't withhold repayment of your debts. Don't say 'some other time,' if you can pay now" (Prov. 3:27,28, TLB). Therefore, before I purchase item two, I pay for item one.

Set Basic Financial Goals

Jesus illustrated this principle when He spoke about the cost of discipleship. He warned:

But don't begin until you count the cost. For who would begin construction of a building without first getting estimates and then checking to see if he has enough money to pay the bills? Otherwise he might complete only the foundation before running out of funds. And then how everyone would laugh! "See that fellow there?" they would mock. "He started that building and ran out of money before it was finished!" (Luke 14:28-30, TLB).

I used to wonder why I could never get ahead financially. Then it dawned on me that I was aiming at nothing. So I set some long- and short-range goals.

(1) Increase our giving.

(2) Get out of debt.

(3) Purchase certain items for the house.

(4) Go on a cash system.

(5) Purchase certain personal wants.

Your financial goals may be entirely different. That doesn't matter. But it is important that you establish your own goals and begin to fulfill them, even if it takes you one, five, ten years, or more.

The results of establishing financial goals have been rewarding. Today my family is experiencing both financial freedom and freedom from guilt. We have the privilege of giving more, which has in turn increased our faith and trust in the Lord. Most of our other goals have been fulfilled and other objectives have taken their places. And God has blessed us abundantly above all that we have asked or thought possible.

This does not mean we are no longer tempted to overspend. Nor does it mean we no longer have to make financial sacrifices. We constantly have to say no to what may seem good at the moment for something better in the future. But life is certainly more livable and enjoyable now that we have commited ourselves to specific biblical principles for managing our finances.

GUIDELINES FOR BUYING

I hope this overview of my own failures and successes in handling money has been helpful. In conclusion I would like to share with you a list of eight questions I try to answer before making a purchase.

(1) Do I really need it?

(2) Is it the best buy?

(3) Should I buy it now?

(4) If it's a luxury (want vs. need), what need am I giving up to buy it?

(5) Can I really afford it?

(6) Will its value last?

(7) What am I really buying? (Prestige . . . a toy . . . something useful?)

(8) Is this a potential barrier between me and God or between me and my family?

As you evaluate your financial situation, determine your problem areas and their causes. As you set new financial goals, let these words motivate you:

Since we have such a huge crowd of men of faith watching us from the grandstands, let us strip off anything that slows us down or holds us back, and especially those sins that wrap themselves so tightly around our feet and trip us up; and let us run with patience the particular race that God has set before us. Keep your eyes on Jesus, our leader and instructor . . . (Heb. 12:1,2, TLB).

6

Why Pray
When You Can Worry?

It was 11:30 Saturday night—too late for me since my typical Sunday begins at 5:30 A.M. Just as my eyes were closing, I heard a loud rumble. The windows rattled, the house shook, and my heart nearly jumped out of my chest. In a flash I was out of bed and my wife was sitting up with eyes wide open.

I shouted, "It's an earthquake! If we get another jolt, hold your pillow over you head and stand in the doorway. I'll check to see if the boys are all right!"

They were still sound asleep. We had only one other minor shake, and so I decided to go back to bed. But I slept little that night, and Sunday was an unusually long day.

The following Saturday, around 10:20 P.M., it happened again. This time our younger son ran into our bedroom and asked anxiously, "Daddy, is that an earthquake?" Amazingly, our older son slept through his second quake.

Although both quakes were mild, their effect on me was detrimental. There was a deeper understanding of my

71

helplessness in the face of such power. Also, for several months I could not escape the crushing sense of anxiety that overwhelmed me, especially on Saturday nights.

Physical safety for family and self is probably one of man's greatest worries. But we also worry about growing old, financial trouble, ill health, personal failure, and our children's futures. In fact, some of us even worry when everything is going well, expecting our blessings to end soon.

Everyone experiences some form of anxiety, even if he can't put his finger on what worries him. In fact, that is the uniqueness of worry. It differs from fear in that fear normally involves an emotional response to a real danger. And fear seldom lasts long. Worry, however, deals with imagined dangers and has been described as "that fruitless activity of the mind which keeps thoughts revolving endlessly with no resulting action." I experienced fear during the earthquake. But afterwards I developed a habit of worrying about potential quakes.

Every generation has had its worriers. This is evidenced by the universal words of Scripture on the subject (see Matt. 6:25ff.; Phil. 4:6). And even though today's worries may seem justifiable, or at least more numerous than in ages past, the biblical injunctions remain and they demand a response.

CAUSES FOR WORRY

We live in a technical age, and because of this our life-styles are fast-paced and full of risks. On the freeways we bet our lives on the ability of ourselves and others who whiz along at a mile a minute in one-and-a-half ton objects. Every year thousands of people lose that bet.

Crime is increasing annually. Muggings, rapes, homicides, armed robberies, kidnappings, hijackings—all are common occurrences. You may live in the ghetto, suburbia, or rural America; it matters not where, there is no escape from these dangers.

Air pollution, water pollution, and *noise pollution* threaten to do in the human race. At the end of 1976, there were more than a half dozen mishaps on the seas involving Liberian oil tankers. Millions of tons of oil were spilled into the ocean. There was a time when you could escape smog, but not anymore. Recently it was discovered that trees in the mountains, six thousand feet above sea level, are affected by smog. You may think that staying inside is the answer, but if there are smokers present, your solution is short-circuited. And finally, many of us live and work in urban centers where the noise levels are deafening.

The *increase of natural catastrophes* tends to make us anxious. In the 1976 earthquake in China, seven hundred thousand people were killed. For many, drought has been another worry. Tornadoes, hurricanes, and floods annually take their toll. These occurrences leave no geographical area untouched; there is no place to hide.

Another major cause of worry is a *misconception of God.* Some Christians are convinced that God does not want them to be happy or successful. They fail to recognize that God is their Father. I know I want the best for my sons; likewise, my Father in heaven wants the best for me! The psalmist wrote about the fulfilled life of one who delights in doing God's will: "And he will be like a tree firmly planted by streams of water, Which yields its fruit in its season, And its leaf does not wither: And in whatever he does, he prospers" (Ps. 1:3). The individual who walks with God will experience prosperity as he fulfills God's will.

Other people believe God has stopped loving them. They believe He hasn't fully forgiven them for some past sin and wants to get even. Where do we get these ideas? Certainly not from Scripture. Man's natural approach to religion is to make God into his own image. And since man does not fully forgive and at times stops loving, he projects this attitude to God and concludes, "God must respond to me in the same way I respond to others."

But the writers of Scripture paint a different portrait of God. Paul wrote, "For I am convinced that neither death, nor life, nor angels, nor principalities, nor things present, nor things to come, nor powers, nor height, nor depth, nor any other created thing, shall be able to separate us from the love of God, which is in Christ Jesus our Lord" (Rom. 8:38,39).

God's forgiveness is just as sufficient as His love. He promises to forget the sins He forgives (Jer. 31:34). David highlights the extent of God's forgiveness by writing, "As far as the east is from the west, So far has He removed our transgressions from us" (Ps. 103:12).

The power of suggestion is still another basic cause of worry. A few months ago I decided to take my family to Disneyland. I was experiencing a tightness in my throat at the time, which I thought might be due to tension caused by increasing pressures at work.

After an exhausting day at Disneyland, we went back to the motel to relax in the Jacuzzi whirlpool shower and crawl into bed. I decided to watch the news before I dozed off. As I listened, I heard a special report concerning the increase of a disease caused in part by intensive X-ray usage in childhood. The disease? Throat cancer!

I couldn't believe what I was hearing. I took this trip to get my mind off work and the problem I was having with my throat. Instead, I now had the hopeless task of getting a good night's sleep while figuring out how many X rays I had had as a child.

About two months after this incident I had another opportunity to experience worry, again caused by the power of suggestion. I had to fly to San Diego on church business. The week before my trip I watched two television movies with my family, one of which involved a skyjacking and the other a plane crash. After seeing these movies, no one in my family wanted me to fly to San Diego, and to be honest I wasn't too excited about the flight myself. Our worried minds were working overtime.

One more cause of worry has to do with *wrong priorities*. Sometimes you may be tempted to place a great deal of emphasis on physical needs. You wonder if you will be able to provide adequately for your family as prices continue to go up. Will you be able to feed them the right kinds of food? Can you provide for their education? Music lessons? Clothes?

Jesus said that unbelievers spend a lot of time worrying about things (see Matt. 6:32), but that Christians should trust God and not worry. God promises to provide for your necessities. If we give God preeminence in our lives, He will give us all we need including those things we spend time worrying about now (see Matt. 6:31,33).

Another misplaced priority involves an overemphasis on work and an underemphasis on the Lord. You may be tempted to be task-oriented rather than God-oriented.

The New Testament offers a perfect example of this

problem. One day Jesus visited his friends Lazarus, Mary, and Martha. Martha immediately went into action for their honored guest. She decided to prepare a meal *par excellence*. She darted from one part of the kitchen to another. But as she made the preparations, she was fuming inside. "Where's Mary? Why isn't she out here helping me?" Finally Martha came to Jesus, where Mary was sitting at His feet, and said, " 'Lord do You not care that my sister has left me to do all the serving alone? Then tell her to help me.' But the Lord answered and said to her, 'Martha, Martha, you are worried and bothered about so many things; but only a few things are necessary, really only one, for Mary has chosen the good part, which shall not be taken away from her' " (Luke 10:40–42).

Martha was interested in doing. But Mary's interest was in learning. Martha saw a job to be done. Mary focused on a Person to know. Martha was task-oriented, while Mary was Christ-oriented.

I have personally discovered that when I spend a lot of time thinking about all the jobs that need my attention, I experience tension. But when I focus my thoughts on the Lord, and spend time with Him, my worries dissipate.

Worry is harmful to your physical, spiritual, and emotional health. Specialists in the field of psychosomatic medicine believe that from fifty to eighty percent of all physical ills originate in the emotions.* Jesus said that worry prohibits spiritual growth (see Luke 8:14).

Therefore, it is imperative that Christians understand how to deal with common worries. The following six principles should prove helpful.

*Cecil G. Osborne, *The Art of Understanding Yourself* (Grand Rapids, Mich.: Zondervan, 1968), p. 41.

CURES FOR THOSE WORRIES

Distinguish Between What You Can and Cannot Control

Some of life's circumstances are beyond your control; others are within your grasp and ability to handle. You can often prevent physical harm, personal failure, and unnecessary problems.

You have the choice of worrying about being involved in an automobile accident or using your seat belt and driving carefully to limit the possibility of an accident or serious injury. You can also decrease your worry about your child's safety when riding his bike at night by making certain he has a good light, good tires, and all necessary reflectors.

Eliminate worry about failure by being prepared for your task well in advance. This includes prayerful planning, consistent practice, and disciplined study. The only time I feared doing poorly on an exam was when I neglected to study.

But what do you do when the circumstances are out of your hands? When your husband leaves on a business trip, or the children go off to school, or your teen-ager goes out on a date, what attitude should you have then? You need to place the situation into God's hands. Although it is beyond your control, the Lord is with your husband, child, or teen-ager. He can provide safety. He can empower them to resist temptation.

Recognize the Futility of Worry

Today there are many "what if" people in the world. They won't try anything new or challenging because they reason, "What if it doesn't work out?" These people also find it difficult to forgive because they question, "What if he does it again?"

Most worry is needless. Studies indicate that of the things we worry about forty percent never happen, thirty percent are beyond our ability to change, twelve percent are needless health worries (like my imagined throat cancer), and ten percent are petty, miscellaneous worries. Therefore ninety-two percent of our worries are unnecessary.

Jesus spoke about the futility of worry when He raised the question "And which of you by being anxious can add a single cubit to his life's span?" (Matt. 6:27). You can worry about your size, your age, mistakes of the past, growing old, and the fact that one day you will die. But worry will not change your size nor prevent any of those events from taking place. Worry is futile!

Live a Day at a Time

This principle has helped me tremendously. I seldom get uptight about any one particular day's schedule. But when I look at my weekly calendar and consider what has to be done in the next two or three weeks, I get that panicky feeling. To eliminate this kind of worry, I now review what I need to do a week at a time and then break those responsibilities into manageable parts and schedule when each should be completed. On Monday I focus only on what has to be done that day and force myself not to think about Tuesday's responsibilities.

If I do otherwise the responsibilities and problems of today coupled with the responsibilities and problems of the next seem overwhelming and little else but worrying about them gets done.

Read how contemporary a two-thousand-year-old statement sounds: "Therefore do not be anxious for tomorrow; for tomorrow will care for itself. Each day has enough trouble of its own" (Matt. 6:34).

You think you have problems today? Cheer up! You will have another batch tomorrow. Just don't dip into tomorrow's problems today. Live one day at a time. Or as Ziggy says, "Why worry about tomorrow. We may not make it through today!"

God Wants You to Enjoy Inner Peace

Some Christians must think God wants them to be miserable, but nothing could be farther from the truth. Isaiah wrote, "Thou wilt keep him in perfect peace, whose mind is stayed on Thee: because he trusteth in Thee" (Isa. 26:3, KJV). Jesus promised His disciples that He would be the supply source for their peace: "Let not your heart be troubled; believe in God, believe also in me . . . Peace I leave with you; My peace I give to you; not as the world gives, do I give to you. Let not your heart be troubled, nor let it be fearful" (John 14:1,27).

Think about the cries of your children when the lights go out at night. "Daddy, Mommy, I'm afraid!" You comfort them and assure them that everything is all right. You whisper, "There's nothing to be afraid of, honey. Now just close your eyes and go to sleep."

You quietly leave the room and everything is peaceful for several minutes. Then the voice calls out again, "Mommy, Daddy, I'm scared of the dark!" Your reaction to those continuous childish worries may vary from situation to situation. But one thing is certain—it is not your desire for your child to worry and cry. You want your child to feel secure and peaceful inside. Your heavenly Father desires that same kind of peace for you. God receives no pleasure when you worry. He wants you to accept His words of comfort and assurance. He wants you to be at peace and sleep well at night. And there is a way to receive His gift of peace.

Claim God's Promises for Yourself

Just as you give your children words of comfort and assurance, God has assured you of His concern for your welfare. Yet it is very easy to ignore His promises.

God encourages you to trust Him for physical protection. The psalmist declared:

I will say to the Lord, "My refuge and my fortress
My God, in whom I trust!"
For it is He who delivers you from the snare of the trapper,
And from the deadly pestilence.
He will cover you with His pinions,
And under His wings you may seek refuge;
His faithfulness is a shield and bulwark.
You will not be afraid of the terror by night,
Or of the arrow that flies by day. (Ps. 91:2-5, italics mine).

Paul rested in God's promise when he was deciding whether he should remain at Corinth or leave the city because of threats on his life. "And the Lord said to Paul in the night by a vision, 'Do not be afraid any longer, but go on speaking and do not be silent; for I am with you, and no man will attack you in order to harm you, for I have many people in this city' " (Acts 18:9,10).

Perhaps you are more worried about your present financial problems than about physical safety. God has given many promises to provide for you financially as you honor Him with your resources.

After the Philippian believers gave sacrifically to Paul's ministry he assured them, "And my God shall supply all your needs according to His riches in glory in Christ Jesus" (Phil. 4:19).

One time I took one of my sons out for dinner and when the bill came I discovered I was fifty cents short. My son came to the rescue by returning part of his allowance to me. When he gave me the fifty cents, he said, "You don't have to pay me back, Dad. Just keep it."

I guess I could have reacted by saying, "You bet I'll keep it. In fact, how much more do you have? I want that too!" But you know, that wasn't my response. I made certain he was not shortchanged in the process. God supplies our needs in a similar manner when we give to Him.

Are you worried about growing old? Think through these truths:

The righteous man will flourish like the palm tree,
He will grow like a cedar in Lebanon.
Planted in the house of the Lord,
They will flourish in the courts of our God.
They will still yield fruit in old age; they shall be full of sap and very green (Ps. 92:12-14, italics mine).

I seldom receive greater blessing than when I visit with older believers. The alertness and vigor of some of them puts me to shame. Often those who have lost their health have a confidence in the Lord and an enthusiasm for His will to be accomplished in them that challenges me to greater faith. Despite old age, they continue to yield fruit.

Many of the Lord's promises lie dormant because no one has claimed them. Develop the habit of taking God at His Word; you will spend less time worrying.

Become a Pray-er

"But I have tried prayer and it doesn't work for me" you say. This is a common rationale for not praying, but it comes from a lack of trust in God. Sometimes after praying about specific problems, I begin to worry about how God will work things out. As I think through the various solutions He might choose, I begin to worry that He will not choose those I like. By this process I mentally box God into my finite thinking pattern.

The hymn writer penned, "Take your burdens to the Lord and leave them there." But at times I find myself taking my burdens to the Lord for His inspection. Then when I think He has seen them long enough (as though He didn't know beforehand), I take them back and worry.

The Scriptures give four very important reasons why I should bring my worries to God in prayer: (1) Because God already knows my needs and worries (Matt. 6:8,31); (2) Because God is able to meet my needs and remove my worries (Matt. 6:26,28-30); (3) Because God wants to provide for me (1 Pet. 5:7); (4) Because prayer produces results (Phil. 4:6,7).

Here is a suggested prayer you may wish to follow as you bring your worries to God:

Dear Father, thank You for caring for me. Thank You for reminding me that You are big enough to handle all of my problems. I'm tired of worrying. I give You my problems and my worries. I will not question how You are going to deal with them. I just thank You that they are now in Your hands. I claim the peace which You promise those who wait upon You. In Jesus' name, Amen.

Why should you pray when you can worry? First, because worry accomplishes nothing profitable. And second, because prayer alone provides the peace you are really wanting.

Don't worry about anything; instead, pray about everything; tell God your needs and don't forget to thank him for his answers. If you do this you will experience God's peace, which is far more wonderful than the human mind can understand. His peace will keep your thoughts and your hearts quiet and at rest as you trust in Christ Jesus (Phil. 4:6,7, TLB).

7

The Superstar Complex

Pride is that sin we can easily recognize in others but rarely notice in ourselves. There are those, of course, who wear their pride with incredible conceit; they spare no effort in letting everyone know they think very highly of themselves.

With most of us, however, pride takes on very subtle forms, and yielding to the temptation of pride is done almost without thinking. Therefore, it is imperative we understand pride to overcome it.

UNDERSTANDING PRIDE

When I lived in Dallas, I often heard an expression that seemed to be a paradox to me. Whenever a Texan received an honor or award he would reply, "I am very proud and humbled to accept this award." That didn't make a bit of sense to me. How could a person be both proud and humble simultaneously? Are they not mutually exclusive?

No, not necessarily. For instance, I am proud of my

sons' abilities, achievements, behavior, and their relationship with my wife and me. As the Bible says, "A wise son makes a father glad" (Prov. 10:1). However, at the same moment I can feel humbled that God has been so gracious to give us boys who are gifted, obedient, and loving. But the pride God hates is that self-centered, self-reliant, self-righteous, and self-glorifying type that controls a person's life-style. No one is immune to pride and as you will see there are many ways pride can gain a foothold in your life.

OBJECTS OF PRIDE

Jesus warned of pride in *religious activity*. He did not denounce giving, praying, and fasting, but He stated that when one performs these religious activities with pride in his heart, the reward is temporal and comes from men alone (see Matt. 6:1–18). Our Lord described the prideful attitudes connected with these otherwise legitimate religious acts: (1) giving alms—to be "honored by men" (Matt. 6:2); (2) praying—"in order to be seen by men" (Matt. 6:5); and (3) fasting—"in order to be seen fasting by men" (Matt. 6:16). A proud man seeks the applause of others, but neglects the God who makes it possible for him to function in life.

The apostle Paul warned about another area of pride—*intellectual knowledge*. He wrote to the Corinthian church: "Knowledge makes arrogant, but love edifies" (1 Cor. 8:1).

The Christian community may have C. S. Lewis, C.E.M. Joad, Francis Schaeffer, or Carl Henry, but in comparison with the world system the church's intellectuals are few. Is this because Christianity is not intelligent? Certainly not. Realistically, it is the only form of religion that makes sense.

Tragically, man's pride in his intellect often keeps him from God. If he accepts God's truth, he then has to give up his own method of personal salvation. He must admit to himself that in spite of his brilliant mind, he is not good enough for God. He must agree with God that he will never find God by intellectualizing his way into heaven. Jesus said, "Unless you are converted and become like children, you shall not enter the kingdom of heaven. Whoever then humbles himself as this child, he is the greatest in the kingdom of heaven" (Matt. 18:3,4).

No, there are not many intellectuals who find Christ. This is why Paul wrote, "For consider your calling, brethren, that there were not many wise according to the flesh, not many mighty, not many noble; but God has chosen the foolish things of the world to shame the wise . . ." (1 Cor. 1:26,27).

Others place pride in their *physical appearance*. Many girls dream of being the beauty queen on campus. There is nothing wrong with that, but they seldom realize the problems that accompany physical beauty. The beauty queen often becomes a mere object of men's lusts. She is dated as a status symbol rather than for herself. Or she may not be dated at all because men are afraid she will turn them down. Added to these problems is the temptation she has of focusing too much attention on her outward beauty. Then as age takes its toll on the outward appearance, her life slowly crumbles before her. By failing to spend time and energy developing her inner character, she misses out on life at its very best.

Have you ever wondered why Lucifer rebelled against God? It wasn't because he wanted to be immoral, nor because he desired greater freedom. Ezekiel related God's reasons for expelling Satan from heaven this way: "Your heart was lifted up because of your beauty; you corrupted your wisdom by reason of your splendor. I cast you to the ground . . ." (Ezek. 28:17).

Material possessions sometimes become objects of pride. The "American dream" is wrapped up in what a person has—a nice house, a nice car, clothes, and money. And for too many Americans this is all their life amounts to—things.

Jesus warned of this philosophy by preaching, "Beware, and be on your guard against every form of greed; for not even when one has an abundance does his life consist of his possessions" (Luke 12:15).

In the Old Testament God warned Israel of the same temptation:

Beware lest you forget the Lord your God by not keeping His commandments and His ordinances and His statutes which I am commanding you today; lest, when you have eaten and are satisfied, and have built good houses and lived in them, and when your herds and your flocks multiply, and your silver and gold multiply, and all that you have multiplies, *then your heart becomes proud*, and you forget the Lord your God who brought you out from the land of Egypt, out of the house of slavery. . . . Otherwise, you may say in your heart, '*My power and the strength of my hand made me this wealth*.' But you shall remember the Lord your God, *for it is He who is giving you power to make wealth* (Deut. 8:11-14,17,18, italics mine).

Pride in material possessions has influenced the middle-class American church by often producing a nauseating complacency and ineffectiveness for the cause of Christ (see Rev. 3:15-17).

One other area of pride affecting the church today centers in *spiritual gifts*. Some Christians are searching for their gift as though they were on a treasure hunt, and they think that until they discover it they will be spiritually useless.

But notice which gifts most believers seek. Often they want the spectacular gifts that are performed in public and noticeable by men. I wish just once I would hear of someone seeking the gift of helps or the gift of showing mercy or the gift of giving. Rather than seeking service gifts, most Christians want performance gifts—teaching, tongues, healing, or leadership. I cannot help but wonder if their motivation is to glorify God or to be seen of men.

Christians may seek recognition by religious activity, intellectual knowledge, physical beauty or ability, material possessions, or spiritual gifts. But the tragedy is they are often unaware of their pride. Instead the typical Christian tends to spiritualize these areas. Here are some examples:

I'm involved in a lot of religious activity because I want to burn out for Christ.

I pursue greater knowledge because I want to defend the faith.

I use my physical beauty or athletic ability to attract people for Christ.

I spend much of my time making money so I can give more to missions, and I want a nice home so the unsaved will be comfortable there.

I want several spiritual gifts so I can serve God more effectively.

Sounds good. But could these statements contain more fiction than fact? Take the following test and rate yourself to determine where you stand between pride and humility.

TESTING FOR PRIDE

In the following series of questions, circle the number that most accurately describes your present attitude.

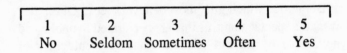

1	2	3	4	5
No	Seldom	Sometimes	Often	Yes

1. It is difficult for me to ask others for help.

1   2   3   4   5

2. I believe that I can handle the routine things of life without seeking God's help.

1   2   3   4   5

3. I believe that I am good enough for God to accept me without receiving Christ as my Savior.

1   2   3   4   5

4. I believe that what I have (money, possessions, abilities, position in life, beauty, intelligence) is mine.

1   2   3   4   5

5. I would have to admit that I find ways to let others know about my abilities, education, and successes.

1   2   3   4   5

6. I honestly believe that I should not have to accept menial jobs in the church (ushering, helping with maintenance, working in the nursery, folding bulletins, volunteer office work, etc.).

1   2   3   4   5

7. If I'm honest with myself, I would have to say I have little interest in those who have not achieved what I have achieved.

1   2   3   4   5

8. I don't enjoy associating with those who are on the low end of the economic, academic, or social scale.

1   2   3   4   5

9. I enjoy special treatment from others and I believe I deserve it.

1   2   3   4   5

10. I prefer being served to serving others.

1   2   3   4   5

Now that you have taken this test, check your score to see where you stand. Where you have circled a 3, 4, or 5, take warning. The higher numbers are indicative of pride in your heart.

You can now check each statement as it relates to

Scripture. (1) 1 Corinthians 12:20-22; (2) John 15:5; Psalm 10:4,11; (3) Ephesians 2:8,9; Romans 3:10-18; (4) 1 Corinthians 4:7; Dueteronomy 8:18; (5) 1 Corinthians 1:29-31; (6) John 13:3-5, 12-17; (7) Philippians 2:3; (8) Romans 12:16; (9) James 2:1-4; (10) Mark 10:42-45.

WHY IS PRIDE HARMFUL?

When a believer persists in pride he does himself no favor. In fact, he *loses fellowship with God*.

Think about the person who constantly brags about his achievements. Do you enjoy being with him? Do you feel refreshed after listening to him tell you how good he is? It is impossible to truly communicate or have fellowship with a proud person. He seems to be interested only in himself. God feels much the same as you do about the proud. "God is opposed to the proud, but gives grace to the humble" (James 4:6).

The only way to experience life at its best is to walk humbly before God. God gave this principle for meaningful living years ago: "He has told you, O man, what is good; And what does the Lord require of you but to do justice, to love kindness, and to walk humbly with your God" (Mic. 6:8).

A second result of pride or even potential pride is *divine discipline*. God's discipline is either corrective or preventive. He corrects me when I disobey Him, but He may also discipline me to keep me from sin.

For instance, I may become wealthy and spend so much time making money that I neglect Him. God might correct me by removing my wealth. On the other hand the Lord could keep me from gaining wealth in the first place and thus prevent the possibility of pride over possessions.

An example of preventive discipline is found in Paul's life. The apostle Paul experienced spiritual reality as few have. His experiences could have led him into a condition of spiritual pride, rendering him useless for God. Paul testifies of God's gracious, preventive discipline: "And because of the surpassing greatness of the revelations, for this reason, *to keep me from exalting myself*, there was given me a thorn in the flesh, a messenger of Satan to buffet me—*to keep me from exalting myself*!" (2 Cor. 12:7, italics mine). No one is certain what Paul's thorn in the flesh was. But the purpose for giving it is certain—to prevent his boasting of his spiritual experiences.

God deals with the proud in still another manner—*forced humility*. Jesus promised, "And whoever exalts himself shall be humbled; and whoever humbles himself shall be exalted" (Matt. 23:12). The political arena was filled with proud men during the early 1970s. They eventually were forced into shame and humility. The United States was humbled when it had to admit to a prolonged, no-victory war in Viet Nam. Great corporations such as Lockheed were publicly humiliated when large payoffs to foreign government officials were uncovered.

One of the greatest biblical examples of forced humility is found in the Book of Esther. Haman had authority over all the king's princes. He loved it when men would bow down as he passed by them. But a Jew named Mordecai refused to bow before Haman. Enraged, Haman was determined to exterminate both Mordecai and his people. But in the providence of God, Mordecai found favor in the eyes of the king, for he uncovered a plot against the king.

The king wanted to honor Mordecai and so inquired of Haman how he should honor someone who pleased him. Haman thought the king wanted to honor him. And so he replied, "For the man whom the king desires to honor, let them bring a royal robe which the king has worn, and the horse on which the king has ridden, and on whose head a royal crown has been placed; and let the robe and the horse be handed over to one of the king's most noble princes and let them array the man whom the king desires to honor and lead him on horseback through the city square, and proclaim before him, 'Thus it shall be done to the man whom the king desires to honor' " (Esther 6:7-9).

The king was pleased with the idea and told Haman to carry out the suggestion immediately. And when Haman learned that Mordecai was to receive the honor, he was humiliated: "But Haman hurried home, mourning, with his head covered" (Esther 6:12).

James points to a further result of pride. He implies that the person who refuses to walk humbly before God *opens himself to satanic attack.* (see James 4:7). When you humble yourself before God, you are placing yourself under God's authority and protection.

When Paul preached in Corinth, he faced a lot of satanic opposition. But God encouraged him by a vision. "Do not be afraid any longer, but go on speaking and do not be silent; for I am with you, and no man will attack you in order to harm you, for I have many people in this city [to obey this command is to place oneself under God's authority and protection]" (Acts 18:9,10).

Enough of the results! What can I do to keep pride from ruining my life? What does the Bible offer me so that I can walk humbly before God and experience a purposeful life?

HOW TO OVERCOME THE SUPERSTAR COMPLEX

Pride is basically an attitude of self-reliance, which can be checked only by developing a biblical perspective of God. *Recognize that God is your supply source.* He supplies you with your money (see Deut. 8:18), your children (see Ps. 127:3), your salvation (see Eph. 2:8,9); your gifts and abilities (see 1 Cor. 12:4–11), and your wisdom (see James 1:5). In fact, everything you have comes from God. "What are you so puffed up about? What do you have that God hasn't given you? And if all you have is from God, why act as though you are so great, and as though you have accomplished something on your own?" (1 Cor. 4:7, TLB).

I must recognize that God has given me everything I have. And He expects me to live as a steward or manager of these things, not as the owner. Therefore I cannot hoard or spend money foolishly as though it belonged to me. I must rather manage it the best I know how. I cannot center my children's lives around my plans for them; they belong to God. I am only responsible for encouraging and guiding them in discovering God's plans for their lives. Nor dare I flaunt my gifts for my own benefit. God gave them to me that I might serve others. And as a steward, I have no other choice but to use them as God provides the opportunity. The more I focus on God's grace to me, the less inclined I will be to pat myself on the back.

Another way to encourage true humility in your life is to *periodically accept responsibility beyond your natural ability*. Complacency can be a deadly enemy to Christian maturity. How long have you taught a Sunday school class, sponsored the youth program, ushered, or sung in the choir? Are you ever challenged to cry out to God and say, "Lord, without you I can't do it. I need your help. I depend upon your Holy Spirit to put life into what I do"?

Sometimes we just need a new challenge, one that we cannot pull off in the power of the flesh, one that will drive us to our knees for help. Writing was that challenge for me. And recently I have accepted a daily radio program. I must confess, I don't even know how to start. But by the time you read this book, that challenge will be history, and I will have to seek other opportunities that will keep me walking humbly before God.

For Solomon, his challenge was ascending to the throne. He cried out to God:

Now, O Lord God, Thy promise to my father David is fulfilled; for Thou hast made me king over a people as numerous as the dust of the earth. Give me now wisdom and knowledge, that I may go out and come in before this people; for who can rule this great people of Thine? (2 Chron. 1:9,10).

Moses was also overwhelmed by his leadership responsibilities:

Moses said to the Lord, 'Why pick on me, to give me the burden of a people like this? Are they *my* children? Am I their father? Is that why you have given me the job of nursing them along like babies until we get to the land you promised their ancestors? Where am I supposed to get meat for all these people? For they weep to me saying, "Give us meat!" I can't carry this nation by myself! The load is far too heavy! If you are going to treat me like this, please kill me right now; it will be a kindness! Let me out of this impossible situation! (Num. 11:11-15, TLB).

Ever feel like that? It could be the challenge of a junior high Sunday school class. It might be the challenge of counseling someone or witnessing to a friend. But whatever the challenge, it should be big enough to keep you on your knees.

Accept Jesus' concept of true greatness. The mark of a truly great man or woman before God is humility, not pride. Jesus told His disciples, after they had argued over who was the greatest, "Whoever wants to be great among you must be your servant. And whoever wants to be greatest of all must be the slave of all. For even I, the Messiah, am not here to be served, but to help others, and to give my life as a ransom for many" (Mark 10:43-45, TLB). God does not equate greatness with how many gifts you have, how intelligent you are, how much money you have made, how attractive you are, or what you have achieved in life. He questions, "Are you willing to serve Me? And by serving Me, are you willing to serve others?"

Peter provides the final principle for fighting the superstar complex: *Humble yourself before God* (see 1 Pet. 5:6). But you may be thinking, "Just how do I humble myself before God?" Here are a few suggestions.

Focus your thoughts on God. The psalmist declared, "When I look up into the night skies and see the work of your fingers—the moon and the stars you have made—I cannot understand how you can bother with mere puny man, to pay any attention to him!" (Ps. 8:3,4, TLB). Psalm 19:1-6 further describes the evidence of God's glory in the heavens. Concentrating on God and His greatness and power helps us to see ourselves in proper perspective.

For instance, when I think about myself, I see big

problems or big success. But when I concentrate on my heavenly Father, I see a big God who has given me success and who will handle my problems.

Depend on Him. Do not call on the Lord only when you find yourself in a real mess. Let God know you need Him just as much for the routine of life. Depend on your Father to supply you with patience when, after having just changed the baby's diaper, he soaks the new one. Depend on the Lord for His love as you rub shoulders with people throughout the day (John 15:5).

Maintain a healthy self-image. God does not want you to be prideful, but that does not mean He wants you to crawl around like a worm and engage in self-abasement. Paul revealed his view of himself in this passage:

For I am the least worthy of all the apostles, and I shouldn't even be called an apostle at all after the way I treated the church of God. But whatever I am now it is all because God poured out such kindness and grace upon me—and not without results: for I have worked harder than all the other apostles, yet actually I wasn't doing it, but God working in me, to bless me (1 Cor. 15:9,10, TLB).

Offer to do the menial tasks at home and at church. Jesus did not feel He was too important to wash dirty feet (see John 13). Yet some Christians feel they are too important to get involved unless they will be publicly recognized or unless the position is "worthy of their stature."

Submit all personal ambition to Him. You may have myriads of goals and objectives for your future. Have you placed them before God and allowed Him to change anything He desires? Why is it that we can trust Him with our life after death, but struggle to trust Him with our life now. A better attitude toward God regarding our futures is reflected in this prayer:

Lord, there are certain things I would like to do in life. I believe that many of these inner desires have come from You. But some are my own and may not be good for me. So I resign my future to You. I want Your daily will for my life. I pray that You will open and close the doors of opportunity according to Your plan. Help me to set goals that will honor You. Keep me sensitive to Your Holy Spirit, so I will be able to understand when You want me to change direction. Above all, help me to keep wanting Your will for my life (see James 4:13-16).

Develop an interest in other people (Phil. 2:4). I have learned that when my thoughts are focused on myself, I develop a leader attitude. But when I think of other people and their pressing needs, I experience a servant attitude. And the essence of real leadership is servanthood.

President Carter shocked the political world when he refused to have "Hail to the Chief" played as he entered a room. Furthermore, he set a new attitude in politics when he reminded staff workers, "We are not your rulers, but we are your servants." A leader who focuses on the honor of his position rarely sees himself as a servant.

Finally, give God the praise for all success. Jesus constantly gave glory to His Father for everything He was doing (see John 5:19; 6:38; 7:16; 8:25-59; 14:10,24).

This does not mean you should refuse to accept an honor from a group of people or a compliment from a friend. If you do refuse, you make it extremely difficult and embarrassing for the one who complimented you. Think for a minute how he feels. If you reply, "Oh that wasn't me; God did it," he may feel you are rebuking him.

It's like saying, "What's wrong with your theology anyway? Don't you know I do nothing of myself? Don't you realize it is God who is working in me?"

Why not say something like this instead: "Thank you very much. I appreciate those kind words. And you and I both know that without the Lord I could never have done it." In your own mind you can tell the Lord, "Father, I know You are the One who has given the success. I praise You for it and thank You for meeting the needs of fellow Christians." This will honor the Lord, and your friend will know you have graciously received his compliment.

Pride—the superstar complex—has become a great barrier between man and God. As long as man insists on self-reliance, he will fail to experience God's best. But if he willingly acknowledges God as the Giver of every good and perfect gift, he will experience God's blessing. Therefore, humble yourself before God and let Him decide who the superstars will be.

8

The Alternative to the Playboy Philosophy

A recent survey in Washington, D.C., showed that more women were having children out of wedlock than in wedlock. Commitment in marriage is rapidly going out of fashion and commitment to an absolute moral standard is as popular in the world as high-heeled sneakers.

You can walk into any drugstore, grocery store, or bookstore and see the latest porno magazine on display in full color. Watch a seemingly innocent television program with your children and suddenly your living room is filled with profanity, innuendos, suggestive dances, or the latest braless fashion.

Anywhere from the college classroom and the business conference to the best-selling novel and the latest hit record, comes the philosophy "if it feels good, do it." The average man on the street may care little about maintaining a high moral standard. But if you are a child of God and desire to please Him, you have but one choice— to live a moral life in an immoral society. Sexual purity is God's will for your life as the Word clearly indicates: "So then, brethren, we are under obligation, not to the flesh, to live according to the flesh . . ." (Rom. 8:12); "Flee immorality" (1 Cor. 6:18); "For this is the will of God, your sanctification; that is, that you abstain from sexual immorality. . . . For God has not called us for the purpose of impurity, but in sanctification" (1 Thess. 4:3, 7).

The world encourages you to look and lust, to do whatever you desire. But the Lord provides an alternative to this playboy philosophy—a life-style of moral purity.

This chapter will answer three major questions: (1) Why does God want me to be morally pure? (2) How can I maintain a life of moral purity? (3) What should I do if I have already engaged in sexual immorality?

WHY MORAL PURITY?

Many individuals, including some misinformed Christians, believe that God put moral rules in the Bible because He didn't want anyone to enjoy life. Dr. Howard Hendricks has been heard to describe this attitude in the following way: One day God hears laughter from earth. Disturbed, He peers over a cloud and shouts, "Hey, what's going on down there?" Man responds, "Just having fun, Lord. We're enjoying life." God angrily retorts, "Well, cut it out. You know that's not allowed!"

God has placed moral laws in Scripture, not to render life a dull drudgery but to allow for true enjoyment. Each of His principles is designed to protect you from missing the best life possible.

God established rules regarding sexual behavior *to protect you physically*. The Bible reveals that the person who lives immorally sins against his own body (see 1 Cor.

6:18). Anyone who has contracted venereal disease knows what this means. And in spite of all the protective measures against VD, the epidemic continues to thrive. In fact, a new strain of gonorrhea has been discovered that does not react to penicillin.

A second reason God established principles of sexual morality was *to protect you emotionally*. Sexual immorality does not enhance emotional stability. The result of disobedience to any of God's moral laws is guilt. And guilt leads to emotional strain. After David committed immorality with Bathsheba he wrote, "When I kept silent about my sin, my body wasted away through my groaning all day long. For day and night Thy hand was heavy upon me; my vitality was drained away as with the fever-heat of summer" (Ps. 32:3,4).

Another biblical illustration of the emotional effects of sexual immorality is seen in Amnon's rape of his half-sister, Tamar (see 2 Sam. 13:1-14). Amnon thought he was madly in love with Tamar. What he desired above everything else was to satisfy his physical desires. He schemed to catch her off guard and then he forced himself upon her. She struggled and pleaded that he not violate her virginity, but Amnon refused to listen.

After he had fulfilled his own physical pleasure the Scriptures record, "Then Amnon hated her with a very great hatred; for the hatred with which he hated her was greater than the love with which he had loved her. And Amnon said to her, 'Get up, go away!' " (2 Sam. 13:15). Of course, Tamar was left feeling disgraced and rejected.

Many steady boy friends and girl friends have experienced a similar emotional reaction. First, there is the passionate expression of love. "I love you. I'll never love anyone else. If you love me, prove it." This verbal expression is accompanied by the touching and caressing of the body. Emotions reach their peak and cry out for total fulfillment. But when it's all over, love is replaced with shame and guilt and the partners may even come to resent each other. God wants to protect you from that type of emotional strain.

God has designed moral principles for another purpose—*to protect you spiritually*. You cannot grow spiritually and live immorally. Sex within marriage is God's will. But outside of marriage it is sin (see Heb. 13:4). The Christian cannot sin successfully. He cannot serve two masters. He must make a choice between his glands and his God. Both cannot control his life.

God also wants *to protect your self-respect*. In spite of all the facades, one thing that prostitutes have in common is an extremely low self-image. When a woman sells her body to a man, she thinks very little of herself. This same principle applies to all of us. Even one unguarded evening can destroy a self-image that has taken years to develop. Someone with a healthy self-image believes, "I'm too important to become a plaything. I am saving myself for the one man/woman that God has chosen for me. Until then, I will date and enjoy the company of the opposite sex. But I refuse to become physically involved."

The Lord has no desire to make you miserable. He wants you to experience a fulfilled life and that is why He included moral guidelines to keep you from hurting yourself physically, emotionally, spiritually, and psychologically. But He has gone further than simply telling you that you must maintain a moral life. He also tells you how to do it.

HOW CAN I MAINTAIN A MORAL LIFE?

Moral living begins with *a commitment to absolute moral standards*. One of the reasons some Christians fail to live a pure life is that they never determine to. They go along with the crowd. They allow their friends and their feelings to set the guidelines.

Have you ever wondered why David failed to resist sexual temptation while Joseph succeeded? I believe the basic reason can be found at this point of commitment. When David had given in to his lusts with Bathsheba, it was not the result of a weak moment. He was merely following a pattern he had already established.

In Deuteronomy 17:17 you can read God's instructions for kings regarding marriage, "Neither shall he multiply wives for himself, lest his heart turn away. . . ." Did David accept God's standard? Not at all. He refused to commit himself to such a rule. Instead, the Bible says, "David took more concubines and wives from Jerusalem, after he came from Hebron; and more sons and daughters were born to David" (2 Sam. 5:13). Therefore, it should not surprise us to read that he lusted after Bathsheba and committed adultery with her (2 Sam. 11:1–5). David apparently had grown accustomed to having what his eyes saw and wanted.

But with Joseph, the story is different. He avoided the advances of Potiphar's wife. Why? Because he was committed to God's moral standard. Notice Joseph's response to an open invitation for sex: "Joseph refused. 'Look,' he told her, 'my master trusts me with everything in the entire household; he himself has no more authority here than I have! He has held back nothing from me except you yourself because you are his wife. How can I do such a wicked thing as this? It would be a great sin against God' " (Gen. 39:8,9, TLB).

Joseph did not follow the standards of Egyptian society. He had normal sexual desires, and at this one moment, he also had the permission of Potiphar's wife and the privacy of a whole house to tempt him to fulfill those desires. But Joseph refused because of his previous commitment to God. His moral pattern was set.

Another way to maintain moral purity is *to avoid long periods of idleness*. The familiar adage "An idle mind is the devil's workshop and idle hands his tools" does not apply only to children. What kinds of thoughts run through your mind when you are just "killing" time or when you have not made a conscious decision to use your time creatively?

A man on a business trip may fill his hours in the hotel watching television or he may wander down to the cocktail lounge and watch a risque show or he may sneak a few girlie magazines up to his room. None of these options will improve his moral life. If he spent those idle periods catching up on personal correspondence, or reading the Word and other Christian literature (see Ps. 119:9,11), he could keep his mind pure.

The married woman who does not work outside the home faces similar choices during her day. She may be tempted to watch the soap operas or the game shows on television. She may eventually find herself "addicted" and turning down opportunities to serve in the church or elsewhere during those times. Or she may feel lonely and seek to escape that feeling by talking with friends on the phone. If she is inclined to engage in gossip, this activity could become a real drag on her spiritual life. As an alternative, the woman with time on her hands could have a neighborhood Bible study in her home or she could do volunteer work at church or in the community.

The young dating couple may face the problem of having too much time alone, which can only lead to trouble. When boredom sets in or late hours lower physical and moral resistance, the glands take over. Therefore, a young couple should plan what they will do on each date and keep decent hours to insure an enjoyable evening.

If you are married, maintain a good sexual relationship at home. When a wife uses sex as a weapon by withholding intimacy, she is doing more than merely frustrating her husband. She is opening the door for Satan to lead her husband to greener pastures. And there is always some woman who will be glad to give a man that which his wife refuses to give. And husbands who have forgotten how to be romantic and sensitive to their wives' emotional needs may be encouraging their wives to seek that kind of consideration from another man.

Paul was well aware of these sexual problems in marriage and his instructions should be heeded:

The man should give his wife all that is her right as a married woman, and the wife should do the same for her husband: for a girl who marries no longer has full right to her own body, for her husband then has his rights to it, too; and in the same way the husband no longer has full right to his own body, for it belongs also to his wife. So do not refuse these rights to each other. The only exception to this rule would be the agreement of both husband and wife to refrain from the rights of marriage for a limited time, so that they can give themselves more completely to prayer. Afterwards, they should come together again so that Satan won't be able to tempt them because of their lack of self-control (1 Cor. 7:3–5, TLB).

Here's a warning for the committed Christian—*look out for those subtle opportunities for sin*. You love the Lord. You have experienced genuine spiritual growth over the past several years. You have no plans to yield to immorality and you find it difficult to understand how any Christian could fall in this way. The Scriptures carry a special warning for you. "So be careful. If you are thinking, 'Oh, I would never behave like that'—let this be a warning to you. For you too may fall into sin" (1 Cor. 10:12, TLB).

If you are a committed Christian man, Satan probably will not be able to persuade you to visit a prostitute. Your resistance is already strong enough to stay away from her enticement. But what about that beautiful Christian gal who is having marital problems and wants your counseling? Or that sweet young thing at the office who thinks you are so masculine and handsome?

As a committed Christian woman, you may have little difficulty shunning the advances of those animal-like creatures at the office, the street corner gang, or the playboy. But how do you deal with that Christian man who is strong but tender, considerate, a man of integrity, attractive—and who has shown you a lot of attention lately? He may be a Bible-study leader, a board member, your best friend's husband, your doctor, or even the pastor of your church. This is the kind of situation you must guard against.

For women only—*dress attractively but modestly*. Some women are really naive in this department. They have no idea how much an exposed female body turns a guy on. Others, however, do know but they enjoy the attention they solicit by their dress. Peter advised, "Don't be concerned about the outward beauty that depends on jewelry, or beautiful clothes, or hair arrangement. Be beautiful inside, in your hearts, with the lasting charm of a gentle and quiet spirit which is so precious to God" (1 Pet. 3:3,4, TLB).

Peter has nothing against outward beauty. But he does recognize that external beauty is temporal while inner beauty is eternal. Although years may decrease the former, they can increase the latter.

An emphasis on inner beauty leads to a chaste and respectful behavior (see 1 Pet. 3:2). But an emphasis on the outer appearance may lead to dress and behavior that cause men to lust after your body (see Matt. 5:27,28). You may think that men are attracted to you as a person, but if you are primarily advertising a body, don't be surprised if you attract those who want a body only.

I don't know who started the lie that the woman is primarily responsible for moral behavior, but don't you believe it. *Men and women are both responsible for moral behavior.*

When dating, some guys put all the responsibility on the girl and then go to great lengths to break down her barriers. If the girl yields to the fellow's advances, he blames her for being too loose. If she refuses him, he thinks she is a prude and explores another field. It is true that a man can be more easily stimulated sexually than a woman, but he also is usually the one to make the advances and in this area he should accept his moral responsibility.

Throughout the Book of Proverbs, exhortations to moral purity are given to men (see Prov. 5:1-21; 6:20-35; 7:1-27). One such instruction reads,

Let your fountain be blessed,
And rejoice in the wife of your youth. As a loving hind and a graceful doe,
Let her breasts satisfy you at all times; Be exhilarated always with her love.
For why should you, my son, be exhilarated with an adulteress,
And embrace the bosom of a foreigner?
For the ways of a man are before the eyes of the Lord,
And He watches all his paths (Prov. 5:18-21).

Another way to maintain a morally pure life is *to control your tongue*. Have you ever realized that an immoral tongue can father an immoral deed? Paul said, "Take no part in the worthless pleasures of evil and darkness, but instead, rebuke and expose them. It would be shameful even to mention here those pleasures of darkness which the ungodly do" (Eph. 5:11,12, TLB).

Paul realized that the more you listen to and repeat stories of sexual exploits and dirty jokes, the greater is the temptation to indulge in them. Jesus, the One who created man (see John 1:3,10), knew the relationship between the heart and the tongue. He warned, "Don't you see that anything you eat passes through the digestive tract and out again? But evil words come from an evil heart, and defile the man who says them. For from the heart come evil thoughts, murder, adultery, fornication, theft, lying and slander" (Matt. 15:17-19, TLB).

I offer one final approach in dealing with sexual temptation: *Recognize that there is no reason to be immoral, only excuses for it*. The kind of excuses I have in mind can be used by both married and unmarried, but they are most often used by the single person.

One excuse for immorality is, "But we love each other!" Usually this means they love each other's body, or they love to gratify their sexual desires. Scripture indicates that love is patient (1 Cor. 13:4). Real love for another person can wait for the proper time and is consistent with God's standards.

"But we already feel as though we are married." This too is an excuse. A good actor feels the part of the character he portrays, but that does not transform him into the actual character. Nor does feeling married actualize the marriage. Put any man and woman who are physically attracted to each other in a bedroom and before long desire for the marriage act will exist. But marriage is not a mere emotion. It is a public commitment of the will for a lifetime relationship with someone of the opposite sex. Then and only then is sex blessed by God (see Heb. 13:4).

Another excuse says, "But it proves that I'm a man/woman." Of course a look in the mirror could accomplish the same objective. Manhood and womanhood include the total person, not just one function of the person. In fact, one of the primary differences between a child and an adult is the ability to control impulses. It is too bad many adults think and behave so much like children, giving in to every desire.

Some excuse immorality on the basis of the supposedly satisfying experiences of others: "My friends don't follow any moral standards and they're happy." Really? I mean, are they really happy? Do they treat each other with respect? Are they free from inner guilt? Is their love the kind that will last forever? The person who brags about his or her sexual exploits may seem happy on the outside, but no one can live free from guilt when they live in sin. This is just another excuse for neglecting God's standards and following selfish desires.

WHAT IF I HAVE ALREADY ENGAGED IN
SEXUAL IMMORALITY?

Perhaps you have already experienced an immoral sexual relationship. You know it was wrong, but you aren't sure what to do about it now.

Start by *confessing your immorality to God*. Agree with God that what you did was wrong. Do not offer excuses to the Lord but admit, "Lord, I have sinned against You. I realize that this was out of Your will. I'm sorry for my sin and claim Your forgiveness" (see 1 John 1:9; Ps. 32:5,8-9,51).

Now *turn away from your past sin and commit yourself to live in accordance with God's moral standards*. "Lord, I turn from my immoral behavior and commit myself to live as You have already shown me from Your Word" (see John 8:11).

Finally, *begin to walk daily in dependence on God's power for moral purity* (see Gal. 5:16). "Lord, I no longer depend on my own strength to resist temptation. But I turn to You and ask You to empower me today to live in moral purity. In Jesus' name, Amen."

You don't have to live in moral defeat. You can experience God's will for your moral life as you continue to rely on Him. And when in doubt about God's ability to help you, remember these words:

And it was necessary for Jesus to be like us, his brothers, so that he could be our merciful and faithful High Priest before God, a Priest who would be both merciful to us and faithful to God in dealing with the sins of the people. For since he himself has now been through suffering and temptation, he knows what it is like when we suffer and are tempted, *and he is wonderfully able to help us* (Heb. 2:17,18, TLB, italics mine).

9

How to Prevent Foot-in-Mouth Disease

"When there are many words, transgression is unavoidable, But he who restrains his lips is wise" (Prov. 10:19). If only we could learn to follow such advice, we would never have to make that futile statement of regret, "I wish I hadn't said that!"

We sometimes open our mouths only long enough to change feet--a tired cliché, yes; but only because it is true. So why do we keep doing it?

CAUSES OF THE DISEASE

Remember the times you told yourself, "I don't know what made me say that. I knew better, but it just came out." What could have caused you to say what you said? Here are some possibilities.

Self-Promotion

This motive shows up in several forms. For instance, consider the *"promises-promises"* approach. Let's say that you enthusiastically agree to accept a certain new responsibility. But circumstances and time pressures soon let you know there's no way you can fulfill that responsibility. You're forced to face the fact that you have to break your promise.

The apostle Peter painted himself into the same corner. Jesus declared that all His disciples would leave Him. Most of the disciples were astonished at the statement, but said nothing. However, Peter could not keep quiet. In his self-confident manner he promised, "Even though all may fall away because of You, I will never fall away" (Matt. 26:33). Quite a promise! Peter promised to be the only faithful disciple. But within hours, this Gibraltar-type he-man crumbled under the threat of Roman arrest. Before the cock crowed, Peter fell away from the Lord, denying Him three times as Jesus had predicted.

Exaggeration is another form of self-promotion. The proverbial fisherman who tells you the size of the fish that got away, the evangelist who reports on the number of decisions at a recent meeting, the person who wants you to know just how gifted he really is—these are all experts at overstatement. "Like clouds and wind without rain is a man who boasts of his gifts falsely" (Prov. 25:14). Have you ever caught yourself stretching the truth just a little to make an impression? That is part of the disease.

Another example of the self-promoter is the individual who tries to *impress others with many words*. He may have a large vocabulary, or he may just be repetitive, but either way he is usually very boring.

Think back to when you were a student facing those blue book exams. Remember when you didn't have the foggiest idea what the professor was asking, but you thought you ought to try to respond intelligently anyway?

So you wrote an epistle in reply, hoping that the prof would take a look at the length of your answer, not bother to read it, and mark you with a superior grade for effort.

Some politicians have developed this approach to promote themselves before the public. They respond to a simple question with many words that seem to form a complex answer, but when you finally figure out what they said, you realize they didn't even answer the question!

Some of the greatest and most important words in history are brief ones. The Lord's Prayer contains 56 words, the Gettysburg Address 266 words, the Ten Commandments 297 words, the Declaration of Independence 300 words. However, a recent government order setting the price of cabbage was found to contain 29,911 words. Need I say more?

Another example of self-promotion is *vulgarity*. You could include swearing and filthy talk in this category, as well as innuendos and dirty jokes. Some people feel the need to be vulgar because it gives them a certain status among their peers. But it has no place in the Christian life-style. Paul admonished the Ephesian Christians saying, "Let there be no sex sin, impurity or greed among you. Let no one be able to accuse you of any such things. Dirty stories, foul talk and coarse jokes—these are not for you. Instead, remind each other of God's goodness and be thankful" (Eph. 5:3,4, TLB).

The Intent to Harm

Threats, curses, slander, destructive criticism, gossip, and sarcasm—all are directed by one person toward another with the intent to hurt him and in the belief that somehow he deserves it.

For instance, sarcasm and criticism are used by one person to belittle another with the hope of elevating himself. This means the attacker already concedes that his victim is more important, more popular, or more successful than he is, therefore, a threat to his self-image. The individual who uses these tactics expresses more about himself than the person he attacks.

Many times when we use sarcasm, gossip, criticism, or some other form of verbal abuse, we are telling the world, "I'm drowning in an ocean of self-pity and I have a poor self-image." We think that by dragging someone else down, we can pull ourselves up. It never works.

The Intent to Cover Up

Sometimes the temptation to lie, withhold information, tell half-truths, or blame others for our failures is yielded to almost unconsciously in an effort to protect our egos or to satisfy our desires.

King Saul took up verbal dancing when the prophet Samuel confronted him with his disobedience to God. God had commanded Saul to destroy the entire Amalekite nation, including the animals. But Saul decided to spare the king of Amalek as a personal trophy and he allowed his army to spare the best animals for their own use.

When Samuel asked Saul to account for his negligence, the king replied, "It's true that the army spared the best of the sheep and oxen . . . but they are going to sacrifice them to the Lord your God; and we have destroyed everything else" (1 Sam. 15:15, TLB).

This answer skirted the issue as did his attempt to justify himself further: "But I *have* obeyed the Lord. . . . I did what he told me to; and I brought King Agag but killed everyone else. And it was only when my troops demanded it that I let them keep the best of the sheep and oxen and loot to sacrifice to the Lord" (1 Sam. 15:20,21, TLB)..

Saul's reasoning was illogical. He was saying it is okay to disobey God (by sparing the animals) as long as you do it to honor Him (with a sacrifice).

The twentieth-century approach is a little more refined than this. We see something we want, but we can only afford it if we don't give as much to the Lord's work this month as last. So we just "borrow" from God, with the intention of not only paying back the money later, but also giving Him a little bonus besides. We try to cover up our disobedience now with promises for the future—promises that are often left unfulfilled.

THE GREAT PHYSICIAN'S PRESCRIPTION

Be Swift to Hear and Slow to Speak

James' response to the problem of an uncontrolled tongue is ". . . be quick to hear, slow to speak and slow to anger" (James 1:19). The normal approach is just the opposite. It's easier to be quick to speak, quick to anger, and extremely slow to listen. That's why we get ourselves into so much difficulty.

Listening quietly means listening creatively. Instead of using my time to dream up arguments for rebuttal, when someone speaks, I must listen with an open mind. I must listen to what the other person is *not* saying as well as to what he is saying. I must "listen" to his body language (eye movement, facial expression, voice quiver, or foot tapping). He may be saying one thing with his words, but communicating an entirely different message with his body ("I'm nervous," "I'm guilty," "I don't know what I'm talking about").

James also implies that I must listen *attentively*. When my wife and children are talking to me, I must turn from the television or newspaper and give them my undivided attention. Otherwise, I may agree to do something that I later fail to do as planned because I did not hear all the details.

Has anyone ever accused you of not listening by saying, "You haven't heard a word I've said!"? If you feel the pinch, develop the art of simple listening.

Develop Restraint Under Strain

I find it easier to put my foot in my mouth when I am tired and under pressure than when I have had a good night's rest and feel invigorated. As the day wears on and the pressures mount, so does the temptation to speak before thinking.

We often feel like lashing out at those who criticize or falsely accuse us. But even though an outburst temporarily relieves the frustration of being under attack, later we usually wish we could have handled the situation more maturely.

I have learned to ask myself several questions when I'm being criticized. (1) Who is the critic? If it is a friend or a person of integrity, I listen attentively. If it is a person who has developed a habit of criticizing, I take it less seriously.

(2) Is the complaint legitimate? Often a
because he lacks information. He m
everything being done to alleviate the
the case, I then attempt to communica
complaint is beyond my ability or responsibility to
remedy, I convey that fact and drop the issue. (3) If the
pressure comes in the form of an accusation, I ask myself
if it is true. If it is, I take the necessary steps to correct the
problem. If it is not, I adopt Paul's response: "I am telling
the truth in Christ, I am not lying, my conscience bearing
me witness in the Holy Spirit . . ." (Rom. 9:1).

God knows my heart, and if I have a clear conscience
before Him, there is no reason to defend myself before
others. Some people would never be satisfied with an
explanation. So I have to accept the fact that God alone
understands and accepts my intentions.

Recognize the Satanic Influence Behind the Problem

How easy it is to forget that we are involved in spiritual
warfare (Eph. 6:12). We can't blame Satan every time we
sin with our tongues, but we should be aware of his
influence.

When Jesus asked His disciples who the people thought
He was, they replied with a variety of public opinions.
Then Jesus narrowed the question to "Who do *you* say that
I am?" Only one man spoke up. He gave the most accurate
description of Jesus given in the New Testament: "Thou
art the Christ, the Son of the living God" (Matt. 16:16).
Jesus told Peter that his answer was a direct revelation
from God.

But a few verses later, the Bible records an interesting

phenomenon. Jesus shared with His disciples that soon He would suffer and be crucified. Elated from his recent eloquent statement, Peter attempted to give Jesus another of his revelations. Only this time his source was not God. "And Peter took Him aside and began to rebuke Him, saying, 'God forbid it, Lord! This shall never happen to You' " (Matt. 16:22). Jesus quickly rebuked Peter in return saying, "Get behind Me, Satan! You are a stumbling-block to Me; for you are not setting your mind on God's interests, but man's" (Matt. 16:23).

How could Peter be so right one minute and so wrong the next? Obviously, his tongue was under God's influence one time and under Satan's the next. The closer one walks with God, the less probability there is of speaking foolishly. However, the reverse is also true.

Realize How Devastating Negative Words Can Be

Remember those unflattering nicknames in school? "Hey fatty!" "There's old cross-eyed." "Hi, Shorty." "C'mon, big ears." "Here comes freckle face." When you combine these with choice comments from parents and teachers ("Boy, are you dumb," "You will never amount to anything," "Blew it again, didn't you"), you have the makings of a giant inferiority complex.

Negative words hurt others, yes, but they also have a way of coming home to roost on the front doorstep. Jesus warned His listeners about careless words: "And I say to you, that every careless word that men shall speak, they shall render account for it in the day of judgment. For by your words you shall be justified, and by your words you shall be condemned" (Matt. 12:36,37).

On August 9, 1974, a U. S. president resigned from office—a first in American history. What brought the president to the point of resignation? The president's own words, recorded for posterity. "By your words you shall be condemned."

The president's words can hardly be justified. But aren't you relieved that there was no tape recorder running while you shared your innermost feelings about a certain person with someone else? Wouldn't you hate to have certain past conversations played publicly? I know I would.

Watergate highlights the seriousness of using words to hurt others. Careless, useless, cutting words not only hurt the one they are directed toward, but also the one who speaks them.

Realize How Profitable Positive Constructive Words Can Be

If negative words can destroy, positive words can build. "Like apples of gold in settings of silver is a word spoken in right circumstances" (Prov. 25:11). "Don't use bad language. Say only what is good and helpful to those you are talking to, and what will give them a blessing" (Eph. 4:29, TLB).

Have you ever wondered how animal trainers teach their animals to respond to command? Certainly not by beating them whenever they make a mistake. They use positive reinforcement—a bit of food, words of praise, or a loving embrace. Some people treat animals with greater love and care than they treat other human beings.

Think of the healthy self-image children would have if parents spent as much time giving honest praise as they do giving criticism. Put confidence, love, and attention into a child's life and you will reap a fruitful harvest. But belittle, nag, and make incessant demands on a child and the harvest will be profitless.

Look for the Positive in People and Circumstances

It takes little genius to see the faults in people and the injustices in circumstances. But it takes God's grace and spiritual maturity to see goodness and potential in people and to be joyous despite unjust circumstances. That is why Paul could rejoice while sitting in a filthy prison cell as the rats raced back and forth. Paul shared his optimism with the believers at Philippi:

And I want you to know this, dear brothers: everything that has happened to me here has been a great boost in getting out the Good News concerning Christ. For everyone around here, including all the soldiers over at the barracks, knows that I am in chains simply because I am a Christian. And because of my imprisonment many of the Christians here seem to have lost their fear of chains! Somehow my patience has encouraged them and they have become more and more bold in telling others about Christ. . . . I am going to keep on being glad, for I know that as you pray for me, and as the Holy Spirit helps me, this is all going to turn out for my good (Phil. 1:12-14,19, TLB).

You may be living in an extremely difficult situation at this moment. Your negative circumstance may be an unsaved husband or wife, or a rebellious child, or debts up to the ceiling. Maybe you feel like screaming. You have prayed that God will change things, but He hasn't.

You have a choice—you can cultivate a negative attitude that will only increase your despair, or you can pray for a positive outlook and be the encouragement those close to you need. As they see your attitude change, they will be challenged to become more positive in their own lives. Jesus said, ". . . with God all things are possible" (Matt. 19:26) and that includes being able to rejoice during tough times.

Maintain a Clean Heart

Probably the most important of all these principles for preventing foot-in-mouth disease is this one. It goes to the root of the problem.

During the summer months in Fresno we have to water our lawns every day. The climate is arid, the temperature usually 100° plus. So when you fail to water, nature quickly takes its course. Therefore, whenever we go on vacation, we invite friends to live in our house. And our friends are very careful not to neglect watering the lawn. In fact, they usually work on the assumption that if some water is good for the lawn, a lot of water is fantastic.

When we return our lawn is always bright green. But something is different—mixed in well with our Bermuda grass is a broad-leafed, dark green water grass.

My first approach to solving the problem is to cut the grass extra short. That way no one sees the water grass for days. But by the end of the week, the ugly broad-leafed grass is all over my lawn again. The only positive solution I have discovered to get rid of this grass is to either spray a chemical that filters down to the root, or pull the grass out by the roots. If the root remains, sooner or later the unsightly weed will show itself again.

So it is with a critical, vulgar, or uncontrolled tongue. You can cover it up for a while. But eventually a circumstance or an individual will catch you off guard and out pours a string of words you wish you had never spoken. Why? Because man has a heart problem. Consider Jesus' words:

A tree from good stock doesn't produce scrub fruit nor do trees from poor stock produce choice fruit. A tree is identified by the kind of fruit it produces. Figs never grow on thorns, or grapes on bramble bushes. A good man produces good deeds from a good heart. And an evil man produces evil deeds from his hidden wickedness. *Whatever is in the heart overflows into speech* (Luke 6:43-45, TLB, italics mine).

I rarely succeed when I try to hide bitter feelings toward someone. Usually my feelings reveal themselves in a cutting or sarcastic remark. My only solution is to come to the Father and pray, "Lord, You know how I feel about that person. I can't hide it from You. I confess my bitter feeling as sin. Please remove the bitterness and love him through me. Help me to see the good in him. And give me words of love to convey the new love You have given me for him. In Jesus' name, Amen."

Once I allow Jesus to deal with the root, He changes the fruit. But when I harbor a root of bitterness (see Heb. 12:15), then I can expect the fruit of destructive remarks.

To conclude this chapter, I've listed seven questions you might ask yourself to determine if and to what extent you might be suffering from an uncontrolled tongue.

TESTING FOR TD (TONGUE DISEASE)

1. Do I normally use words as a weapon to destroy rather than a tool to build (Eph. 4:29)?
2. Do I usually focus on problems rather than on the opportunities (Num. 13:30–33)?

3. Do I believe that my greatest contribution to others is telling them how bad they really are (Matt. 7:3-5)?
4. Do I believe that I'm an authority on most subjects (Rom. 12:3)?
5. Do I believe that the best way to settle an issue is to tell people off (Prov. 29:11)?
6. Do I believe that an uncontrolled tongue is just a small weakness rather than a real sin (James 3:5-12)?
7. Do I believe that I should always express my views before someone else expresses his (Prov. 18:2,13)?

If you answered several of these questions with "yes," you had better go to the Great Physician and ask Him to remove the root problem. Otherwise, you may spread the germ to others until your family and friends become infected.

Quietly take time with your Father in heaven. Let Him know where you hurt. He understands your hurts and will graciously bring healing to your heart so that you will be free from the destructive use of your tongue. Then you can become the one that encourages others to give thanks rather than to complain, to praise instead of to ridicule.

10

Crowd Pleaser
or Pacesetter?

The new President wore a sweater as he sat by the fireplace. Looking into the TV camera, he encouraged millions of Americans to set their thermostats at the same setting as those at the White House—a cool 65°. Whatever your political persuasion, you must admit that among other qualities, Jimmy Carter is a pacesetter.

Civil rights advocates saw another pacesetter, Martin Luther King, climb his mountain and declare, "I have a dream." Several years ago consumers watched an aggressive young man confront big business, like a David facing a Goliath. Within months, Ralph Nader became a household word.

Centuries ago the nation of Israel heard one of its own men challenge, "If you are unwilling to obey the Lord, then decide today whom you will obey. . . . But as for me and my family, we will serve the Lord" (Josh. 24:15, TLB).

A pacesetter is one who by example or other means of persuasion goes against the tide of public opinion to set a new course of belief or action. There are not too many pacesetters among us, probably because it is easier to follow the crowd than to risk ridicule for being different. But generally the decision to agree with public opinion or to defend the status quo is influenced by various factors, eight of which will be discussed here.

HOW DO YOU MAKE YOUR DECISIONS?

One of my worst decisions in high school was choosing a free study period over world history. I enjoyed the world history class the two times I attended, but a friend convinced me the course would become more difficult as time passed. So I canceled the class, substituted a study period, and then neglected to use that time for study. Convenience became more important than education; I had chosen the *easy route*.

Some people make decisions based on *tradition*. Like an old friend, tradition provides us with a sense of security and familiarity. You probably know someone who is so accustomed to the way his church handles the order of worship on Sunday mornings that he becomes uncomfortable in or even critical of other worship practices. This person may sincerely believe that his preferences are based on the scriptural instructions for worship rather than on the traditions of his denomination. A study of New Testament worship practices, however, would dispel this notion. The average worship service today has little in common with those first-century services.

Tradition is not necessarily bad, especially if its function is biblically based. However, we should not hold on to traditions when they have outlived their meaningfulness and have proven a hindrance to spiritual growth.

Peer group pressure and a desire for popularity and acceptance greatly influence our decisions. Watching my sons as they enter adolescence has been a joyful experience. They once had no concern if they went to school with faces stained by grape juice, hair standing up, or wearing shirts that clashed with their trousers. But they have changed. Now the face is carefully checked in the mirror, the hair is just right, and the clothes match. Why? Peer pressure—the do-as-everyone-else-does attitude.

Peer pressure is helpful when it encourages better grooming, but it causes conflict when it challenges moral and spiritual decisions. The Christian teen-ager must constantly choose between pleasing God or his friends. The young adult feels pressured to own his own home, drive a late model car, and have all the conveniences his friends are buying on the installment plan. Commitment to attain certain economic and vocational goals often conflict with commitment to Christ and His church.

A fourth aspect of decision-making is the *concern for personal gain*. What will give me the greatest benefit? What am I going to get out of it? This attitude can be contrasted with Paul's exhortation to the Philippians: "Don't be selfish; don't live to make a good impression on others. Be humble, thinking of others as better than yourself. Don't just think about your own affairs, but be interested in others, too, and in what they are doing" (Phil. 2:3,4, TLB).

Here are the questions one usually considers when making a decision: (1) What is convenient? (2) How have I done it before? (3) What will cause people to like me? (4) What are the personal benefits? These questions are obviously self-centered.

The question that needs to be raised is *What is right?*

Paul told the Corinthians, "Our responsibility is to encourage the right at all times, not to hope for evil. We are glad to be weak and despised if you are really strong. Our greatest wish and prayer is that you will become mature Christians" (2 Cor. 13:8,9, TLB).

Paul was not a traditionalist. He seldom did what was popular. He refused to find an easy way to gain converts (2 Cor. 4:2), and he had no desire to please only himself (Rom. 15:1,2). Paul refused to follow the crowd. He knew what had to be done and he set out to reach his objective. The apostle could say with confidence, "I exhort you therefore, be imitators of me" (1 Cor. 4:16).

Another factor that influences us to follow the crowd is our *majority rules* philosophy of life. When an individual does not conform to what the majority has decided is right, most people feel something must be wrong with him. Yet the Scriptures clearly demonstrate that the majority is not always right.

The majority in Moses' day decided not to enter the Promised Land, and because of that decision the entire nation suffered for forty years in the wilderness (Num. 13:30-14:35). In Jesus' day the majority cried out, "Crucify Him! Crucify Him!" Jesus Himself indicated that public opinion would reject His way of salvation: " 'Heaven can be entered only through the narrow gate! The highway to hell is broad, and its gate is wide enough for all the multitudes who choose its easy way. But the Gateway to Life is small, and the road is narrow, and only a few ever find it' " (Matt. 7:13,14, TLB). In moral and spiritual issues the majority is usually found disagreeing with God's standards.

Individuals refuse to become pacesetters for another reason—*the fear of men*. We may ask ourselves, What

will people think? or What will they say if I do that? or
How will they react if I take an unpopular stand? "The
fear of man brings a snare, but he who trusts in the Lord
will be exalted" (Prov. 29:35).

A *lack of personal conviction* places a person at the
mercy of every wave of public opinion that comes along.
Many Christians carry their parents' beliefs with them
until they are challenged by an alternate point of view.
Others ask, "What's wrong with just a little drink?" Or
they say, "A little pot never hurt anyone!" or "Everyone
hedges on his income tax now and then!" or "C'mon, you
won't lose your salvation by going to R-rated movies.
Let's see how the rest of the world lives!" At times like
this, it is tempting to lay aside parental beliefs and try
something a little risque! That is why the Bible urges,
"The faith which you have, have as your own conviction
before God" (Rom. 14:22).

Someone once wrote that a belief is something you
hold, but a conviction is something that holds you. Your
beliefs must become your convictions if they are to have
any value at all. You may believe God answers prayer, but
do you know this as a fact? If not, begin to consistently
pray for specific requests and record God's answers. You
may believe Jesus saves from the penalty of sin, but you
are not delivered from the guilt of your own sin until you
open your heart and allow Christ to enter your life. You
may believe the Holy Spirit empowers Christians to live
fulfilled lives, but only as you allow Him to control your
life daily will this belief become your conviction.

The *peace at any price* philosophy also contributes to
conformity. A wife becomes a "secret service Christian"
because she doesn't want to disrupt her family life. A
teen-ager keeps his conversion experience a closely

guarded secret because disharmony could erupt in his gang if they discovered the truth.

God wants man to experience peace, but not at the price of denying the gospel or disobeying God. When Paul preached Christ at Ephesus, the entire city was in an uproar (Acts 19). Jesus Himself preached,

"Don't imagine that I come to bring peace to the earth! No, rather, a sword. I have come to set a man against his father, and a daughter against her mother, and a daughter-in-law against her mother-in-law—a man's worst enemies will be right in his own home! If you love your father and mother more than you love me, you are not worthy of being mine; or if you love your son or daughter more than me, you are not worthy of being mine. If you refuse to take up your cross and follow me, you are not worthy of being mine" (Matt. 10:34-38, TLB).

The average person will go out of his way to avoid an argument—sometimes because he is afraid of offending another, but more often because he can't defend what he believes. And so he goes through life being very careful not to rock the boat. This attitude is not Christ-like. Jesus argued with the religious leaders of His day and sometimes used strong language to expose falsehood (Matt. 23:13-36). Paul was not intimidated by those in authority when he knew they were wrong (Acts 23:3). Peter refused to yield to the demands and threats of the Jewish leaders when they told him to live contrary to God's will (Acts 5:28,29). God wants us to live at peace with others, but not at any price. Peace should never be fulfilled at the expense of obeying the will of God.

Your responses to the following statements should help you see if you are a conformist or a pacesetter. Evaluate yourself honestly and underline your responses.

AM I A CROWD PLEASER OR PACESETTER?

1. I feel self-conscious giving thanks for food in a public restaurant. (Yes—No)
2. I have difficulty graciously refusing alcoholic beverages offered by friends and associates. (Yes—No)
3. I cannot go against tradition, even if a change is better. (Yes—No)
4. I make most of my decisions on the basis of what others may think or say. (Yes—No)
5. I am afraid to disagree even though I know the other person is wrong. (Yes—No)
6. I usually go along with the majority opinion, no matter what it may be. (Yes—No)
7. I am willing to overlook something I know is wrong in order to keep everyone happy. (Yes—No)
8. I must admit that my friends more often influence me for bad than I influence them for good. (Yes—No)

God wants you to be a pacesetter rather than a crowd pleaser. You may have to forfeit peace in your family for awhile and it might cost you some of your friends. Perhaps you won't be able to achieve that position and salary for which you've been striving. Pacesetting is costly. But it is God's will for you.

HOW CAN I BECOME A PACESETTER?

Much of what you do depends upon your frame of reference. A photographer friend invited me to his house one day to evaluate a photo. It was good, but nothing spectacular. Then he placed the photo in an expensive frame and again asked me how I liked it; I replied, "Fantastic!" The picture was transformed from good to fantastic with the addition of a frame worth about five times the price of the photograph.

In a similar way public opinion places an exciting frame around sin to highlight the pleasures and hide the consequences. But if you look at God's frame of reference revealed in the Bible you will see *sin* for what it really is—a life-style apart from God, resulting in spiritual death and unfulfillment.

Therefore, learn to *interpret life from a biblical frame of reference*. Ask yourself questions like these before making a choice: "How does my decision measure up to God's standards?" Will it please Him? Is it moral? Is it ethical? Will it help or hinder my Christian testimony? Is it beneficial for others?

A second part of becoming a pacesetter is to *realize that God has called you to set the example for others*. This is not an option. Jesus said that you are salt (Matt. 5:13). Therefore, help make your peer group tasteful. Season your conversations with positive, encouraging comments and maintain the standards you know are right. Jesus also calls you to give spiritual light to those living in darkness (Matt. 5:14-16). You are also likened to a city set on a hill; therefore be conspicuous but not obnoxious. Confess Jesus before men (Matt. 10:32,33) and do not conform to the world's standards (Rom. 12:2). Refuse to become a crowd pleaser (Gal. 1:10), for your calling is to be a pacesetter. As you allow this fact to grip your heart, you will be the one whom others follow.

Now that you are aware why God has called you to Himself, *determine to serve Christ rather than the crowd*.

Jesus taught that no one can serve two masters (Matt. 6:24), but many Christians are trying anyway. Some attempt to live for money and for Christ simultaneously, gaining nothing but frustration in the process. Others seek to build God's kingdom, but end up building their own. Some believers become so entangled in the pleasures of the world that they spend little time with the Lord. Realize that time and energy have limitations. If these resources are spent in the pursuit of worldly pleasures and riches, and on the anxiety produced from that pursuit, then God receives nothing but leftovers. The result is a fruitless life (Mark 4:19). In contrast to this futility, adopt a life-style that reflects true commitment to Jesus Christ. Decide once and for all to play on His team.

If a quarterback is losing badly, he may wish he were playing on the other team. But it's incredible to imagine a quarterback playing the first half of a game for his team and the second half for his opponents. The rules of football don't allow it.

Nor do the rules in the game of life. Yet many Christians make a gallant attempt to accomplish the impossible—to live part of their lives for Christ and the other part for themselves. Decide whom you will play for and then commit yourself to that team. Your commitment determines your life-style, and your life-style either conforms to what everyone else does or sets the pace for others to follow.

Expect opposition in life and learn to deal with it in a Christ-like way. Sometimes Christian leaders mislead potential believers by telling them that the Christian life is one of peace and prosperity. There is truth in this, but the Bible also teaches that those who follow Christ uncompromisingly can expect opposition. Also, God sometimes chooses to use difficult circumstances to teach us and to help us grow. Jesus said, " 'The world would love you if you belonged to it; but you don't—for I chose you to come out of the world, and so it hates you. Do you remember what I told you? "A slave isn't greater than his Master!" So since they persecuted me, naturally they will persecute you. And if they had listened to me, they would listen to you!' " (John 15:19,20, TLB). Peter gave a similar warning to his readers (1 Pet. 4:1-5, 12-19). Becoming a Christian does not solve all personal problems. But it does provide One who will be with you through your problems.

Therefore, when your friends make fun of you or avoid you because of your faith, remember: This is God's confirmation that your life is conforming to His will rather than to the world's pattern.

Do some pacesetting this week. Take the initiative to influence someone for good. Maybe there is a problem at the office, at home, or at school. People are being hurt because everyone is ignoring the problem. Don't you think it's about time *you* do something about it? Carefully think through a possible solution, then share your plan of action with a trusted friend. Bring the solution to the Lord in prayer and as He leads step out in faith and act.

Or maybe you could set the pace for other Christians by telling a friend about Jesus. Many believers would willingly share Christ with others if they could see how it's done.

You can be the pacesetter God wants you to be. As you discover ways to assume this role, ask God to give you the courage to stand out—not like a sore thumb, but as a city set on a hill.

11

I Need a
Twenty-five-Hour Day

You live in a busy world. Your children may be involved in organized sports, music lessons, and church and school activities. As a mother, you may spend most of your time playing taxi for your children, attending various Bible studies and church activities, as well as keeping up with the never-ending housework. If you are the man in the family, you have your job, family responsibilities, hobbies, and other activities.

With so much activity and so little time, you may sometimes want to scream, "I need a twenty-five hour day!" But is lack of time really the problem?

MAJOR TIME PROBLEMS

The three most common time problems you probably face are wasted time, procrastination, and overscheduling.

Wasting time means using time for unprofitable purposes. Why do people waste so much time? One reason is because they can think of nothing better to do. They have no goals or priorities and therefore aim at nothing. They live on the level of feelings, doing what they feel like doing. Others waste time because they are indecisive, they lack schedules, or they do things haphazardly.

A second time problem is procrastination—the I'll-get-it-done-tomorrow attitude. When I procrastinate, it usually involves those jobs that should be done, but are not high on my priority list. They usually include work around the house, such as mowing the lawn, painting, and fixing odds and ends. You may find yourself easily putting off those difficult jobs or the unexciting, routine ones.

The third problem is overscheduling, which involves cramming too much activity into too little time. The traveling businessman may accept appointments too close together, not allowing time for travel. The busy homemaker may speak at a luncheon, attend a women's Bible study, take the children to their music lessons, clean house, and fix supper all in the same afternoon. The Murphy's Law mandate "Whatever can go wrong will go wrong" usually goes into effect at such times.

If you do not identify with all of these time problems, you should share your secret with the rest of us. However, if you are a fellow time-waster, procrastinator, or overscheduler, you may want to learn about effective time management.

BASIC ASSUMPTIONS REGARDING TIME

Assumptions are the foundation stones; principles are the actual building blocks. So before I share the biblical principles for effective time management it is important to understand what I am building on.

I first build upon the fact that *time belongs to God. I am but a steward (manager) of God's time.* The psalmist affirmed, "My times are in Thy hand" (Ps. 31:15). Daniel testified that time belongs to God: "And it is He who changes the times and the epochs" (Dan. 2:21). Time in this sense is like money. You can spend it for your personal pleasures and squander it, or you can invest it in the lives of others and use it for God's purposes. God holds you accountable for your choice.

The second assumption is *God will never give you too much to do.* You may overschedule yourself. You may use a full schedule to relieve personal guilt, to impress a boss, to escape family problems, to protect yourself against boredom, or for some other reason. Other people may ask you to do more than is humanly possible, but God will not. Solomon wrote, "There is an appointed time for everything. And there is a time for every event under heaven" (Eccles. 3:1).

Ask yourself these questions: (1) Must I do all that I have scheduled in the time I have allotted for it? (2) Does God want me to finish all of this work in the time I have allowed for myself? (3) Does God want me to do all that I am trying to do?

I've discovered over the years that I'm my own worst enemy when it comes to a schedule. My responsibilities include preparation for preaching and teaching, counseling opportunities, administrative responsibilities, visitation, discipling men, radio programming, and writing. The problem I always face is how to get it all done in the least amount of time. No one in my congregation has set up a schedule that says, "First do this, then that, followed by those other tasks." Therefore, I have to decide how much time to allot to each responsibility. So I constantly ask myself, "What does God expect from me?" "What are His priorities for these responsibilities?"

Closely associated with this assumption comes a third foundation stone—*God equips you to do what He has assigned for you*. Do you have a problem with accepting responsibilities for which you have no training, natural skill, or spiritual gift? God does not ask you to do what seems impossible to you unless He also provides the ability. You may be frustrated at this moment because you know you are trying to do something you can't handle adequately. Do you believe God wants you to keep that position or responsibility? Is God's work being helped or hindered because of your involvement? Are people being blessed or frustrated because of your own frustrations or attitudes?

Remember Paul's exhortation to the Roman Christians:

And since we have gifts that differ according to the grace given to us, let each exercise them accordingly: if prophecy, according to the proportion of his faith; if service, in his serving; or he who teaches, in his teaching; or he who exhorts, in his exhortation; he who gives, with liberality; he who leads, with diligence; he who shows mercy, with cheerfulness (Rom. 12:6-8).

God has equipped you to function effectively according to your spiritual gifts. When you go out of your realm of expertise, you not only frustrate yourself, but you also rob another believer of the opportunity to exercise his gift for the Lord. (See my book, *Discover Your Spiritual Gift and Use It*, Tyndale House, 1974.)

We can also assume that *each person has the same amount of time*. You and I have the same daily amount of time as the president of the United States, Billy Graham, and the president of General Motors. But when you compare what you accomplish in twenty-four hours with what others accomplish in the same period, you may discover quite a contrast.

Since you are not the president, God does not expect you to do all that is required of one. But are you using your time effectively in that to which He has called you?

Student, how are you using those free hours between classes? How about your evenings? Housewife, how much time do you waste on the soap operas and game shows? Working woman, how do you spend your evenings after a hard day at work? Man, what do you do with the many interruptions, long lunches, office chitchat, evening at home, and weekends? Are you using your time so that you not only finish your daily assignments, but also are free to invest time with your family, church, and personal hobbies?

These questions lead into the fifth assumption. *Each person needs to use his time efficiently (doing the right things) and effectively (doing things right)*.

Efficiency is doing what needs to be done and doing it at the right time. I was not very efficient during my first year of college. Almost all my time outside of class was spent playing ping-pong, visiting friends in the dorm, and just plain goofing off. Obviously, I should have been studying most of that time.

Effectiveness is how well one does the right things. I decided to study more often during my second year at college, but since I had not yet established good study habits I was doing the right things in a poor way. It took another year before I became both an efficient and effective student.

Are you doing what you should be doing? Are you striving for excellence in what you choose to do? Efficiency-Effectiveness: two basic objectives which should become part of your time management program.

I also build upon the fact that *when you use time you choose to include and exclude simultaneously*. You are now reading this book, and in the process you are excluding other things from this time period. You are always choosing how you will spend your time. You may begin your day with the Lord, giving up an extra fifteen minutes of sleep, or you may exclude the Lord and gain a few more minutes of sleep (see Prov. 6:9–11). The choice is yours.

Here is another assumption to consider: *Doing anything well takes time*. I have often heard people say "God never expects any of us to be perfect," which reflects an attitude that usually translates into poor effort. The results? Soloists sing off-key, choir members don't harmonize well, church boards make poor decisions based on inadequate information, Sunday school teachers attempt to "play it by ear," and preachers bore their congregations with shallow sermons week after week.

Does the Bible tell us that God does not expect us to be perfect? Read what Jesus said in Matthew 5:48: "Therefore you are to be perfect, as your heavenly Father is perfect." True, we will not actually be perfect until we are in the presence of the Father, but He expects us to strive for perfection now by doing our best for Him.

Most people want their efforts to produce good results,

but often they are unwilling to put in the time and effort necessary to realize their desire. Before Jesus began His ministry He spent three years in preparation. His disciples spent three years in intensive training before they were ready to lead the church. The apostle Paul spent nearly fourteen years studying and growing in his spiritual life before he went on his first missionary journey. Paul was not putting off what he knew had to be done; rather he was aware that without proper preparation his efforts would not be as effective as he wanted them to be.

There are times when you must settle for limited objectives. You may not always be able to give your best shot, but you can strive for excellence within unavoidable limitations (see Phil. 1:10).

Also consider this: *some things are not done because of lack of interest rather than lack of time*. How often have you turned down a responsibility saying, "I'm sorry, I just don't have time," when you really meant, "I'm just not interested."

There are many things I know I could be doing and maybe should be doing. But truthfully, they don't interest me. They may be good and necessary, but my interest lies elsewhere. Reasons for lack of interest probably include, (1) the task is too difficult; (2) it is not challenging enough; (3) I have tried it before and failed; (4) someone might do it better than I; (5) it takes more time than I feel it is worth; (6) I wouldn't know where to begin; (7) I have more important things to do; and (8) it will cost me too much to get involved.

Here is my final assumption—*the urgent is seldom important and the important is seldom urgent*. Moses discovered this truth out in the wilderness. He was spending long hours judging the people's disputes:

And it came about the next day that Moses sat to judge the people, and the people stood about Moses from the morning until the evening. Now when Moses' father-in-law saw all that he was doing for the people, he said, "What is this thing that you are doing for the people? Why do you alone sit as judge and all the people stand about you from morning until evening?" (Exod. 18:13,14).

Moses explained to his father-in-law that he was the only one who could tell the people how to handle their problems according to God's law. Jethro encouraged him to delegate his *correcting* responsibilities to others and begin a more important personal ministry—*preventing*. Moses could prevent a lot of the problems by teaching the people God's law. Jethro said, "Now listen to me: I shall give you counsel, and God be with you. You be the people's representative before God, and you bring the disputes to God, then *teach* them the statutes and the laws, and *make known* to them the way in which they are to walk, and the work they are to do" (Exod. 18:19,20).

How often is your train of thought interrupted either by making or receiving telephone calls? They may seem urgent at the time, but they probably are unimportant and could be put off until later in the day. I recently read an article suggesting that business people return phone calls between 11:30 A.M. and 12:00 M. and 4:30 and 5:00 P.M. The one who called you will either want to go to lunch soon or go home; therefore the conversation will focus on the business at hand and will eliminate chitchat.

Some matters that seem urgent will actually take care of themselves given enough time. A problem that has stirred up the emotions of those involved is best dealt with when objective, rational thought is regained.

With the conviction that these nine assumptions are

valid, I can now introduce the principles that when applied can help you avoid wasting time, procrastination, and overscheduling.

KEY ISSUES FOR TIME MANAGEMENT

Evaluation

This is the place you must always begin when considering change. What am I doing with my time? How am I using it?

Take a piece of paper and divide your day into three segments: morning (8—12), afternoon (12—5), and evening (5—10). Think back to yesterday. List the activities you did during each segment. Next to those activities that were essential, place the letter E. By those that were fairly important, place an F. Place a W by the activities that were probably a waste of time. Now follow the same procedure for each day for the past week. Count the number of E's, F's and W's and you will have a pretty good picture how you are using your time. You will also discover what period of the day you tend to waste more than others.

A second way to evaluate your time is to begin with a list of the previous day's activities and then ask yourself, "Which of these tasks could I delegate to someone else?" Parents can delegate many household responsibilities to older children. This helps the parents and develops a sense of responsibility in the child. A job I have recently turned over to my sons is yard work. They do the mowing and raking while I trim and add the finishing touches.

Husbands can delegate certain responsibilities to their wives, and wives may do the same, perhaps by asking their husbands to stop at the grocery store on their way home from work. Once you lift delegation from the boss-worker concept, you will enjoy the cooperation of other family members and friends.

Goal Setting

A second important issue in time management is goal setting. Evaluation primarily asks, "What am I doing?" Goal setting wants to know, "What should I be doing and why?" Perhaps as you were evaluating your present use of time, you came to the conclusion that you waste too much time. In order to use time more profitably you should establish some clearly defined goals.

Relationship goals determine how you are going to spend more time developing your relationship with the Lord, with your family, and with other people. *Task goals* are those jobs that you want to do or must do. At the beginning of each week I list my task goals. They include preparing for Wednesday's family night Bible study and the Sunday morning and evening messages. I might also decide to write a chapter of a book. Next, I consider my relationship goals. This includes specific ways I can develop my relationship with the Lord, my family, my staff, members of the congregation, and those outside the church.

Another goal category requires that I ask myself which of my tasks truly fall into my realm of *ability and responsibility*. I may be responsible for many things, but able to do only a few. Therefore, I delegate some jobs to others who can handle them better or who have more time to devote to them.

Finally, I list the *priority goals*. I divide my tasks into four areas: (1) Essential, (2) Important, (3) Good, (4) If time permits. If I am asked to do something that would not allow me to complete the top priorities, I politely decline, or when something unexpected but important comes up I rearrange my priorities.

Planning

Nothing is more frustrating than trying to do an assignment or complete a task at the last minute. Home Bible studies, Sunday school classes, youth programs, and other activities suffer greatly from poor planning.

One of the best investments you can make is a yearly calendar with plenty of writing room. We have one at home for scheduling social events, and one at my office for business purposes. I also carry an appointment calendar in my pocket.

God is not a God who does things on the spur of the moment. Yet many Christians believe it is unspiritual to plan ahead and work on a schedule.

God established His plan for the ages in eternity past. He works according to a divine plan, a truth revealed in Scripture: "this Man, delivered up *by the predetermined plan* and foreknowledge of God, you nailed to a cross by the hands of godless men and put Him to death" (Acts 2:23, italics mine). "For indeed, the Son of Man is going *as it has been determined* . . ." (Luke 22:22, italics mine).

If God works on an eternal plan, why can't believers work on a monthly, quarterly, yearly, and five-year plan? True, the plans must be flexible. New facts will be discovered and new ideas presented which will alter the plan. But at least a plan will get you going in the right direction. Once you decide what you will do, plan a time sequence for your activities. This becomes your schedule.

You may schedule your time *according to importance*. What items must I do this morning and which ones can wait until later in the day? You can save time (and money) by doing errands according to *geographical location*. If the grocery store and your child's music teacher are in the same part of town, do your grocery shopping while he has his lesson.

A third consideration is to schedule yourself *according to alertness*. I find that I'm most alert in the mornings between eight and twelve and least alert between two and five. Therefore, mornings are better used for mental activity (study or creative planning) and afternoons for physical activity (visitation or meetings that involve some travel). Do your creative tasks when you are most alert.

If you have devised a plan and a schedule don't neglect to use them. If you don't follow your schedule, your effort has been futile.

Time-savers

Use your time twice. You have seen jugglers in the circus who can keep as many as eight balls moving through the air simultaneously. Some people, like jugglers, can do several things at one time.

You can often do at least two things at a time. For instance, as you drive your car you can listen to Bible teachings on cassette tape. Whenever you have to wait (at the doctor's office or in the beauty shop), you can read a good book, plan your day, or write letters. My wife has knitted several beautiful afghans by carrying her knitting to the homes of friends when she knows she will be sitting and talking.

Another important time-saver is to *do your work right the first time*. How often have you found yourself taking shortcuts and neglecting details, only to discover that the job has to be done over?

Thirdly, *salvage your time*. That is, snatch an hour from something you do out of habit, but is not highly profitable. For instance, instead of watching television all evening, turn it off and do something more useful or creative. Sometimes the TV set in my house is silent until eight o'clock. Until then we read, play games, talk to each other, or do a number of other things more profitable than watching television.

Maybe you can get by with less sleep. You may work as well on seven hours of sleep as you do on eight. Find out what is best for you. If you can snatch some time from your sleep, you may discover something quite useful to do with that extra time. It could be used for Bible study, prayer, extra reading, Sunday school preparation, recreation, exercise, or many other valuable activities.

Another way to save time is to take advantage of creative moments. I have already suggested that certain times of the day are more creative than others. But I refer now to those times when you are inspired to do something useful outside of the normal routine.

One Sunday my wife and I went out to a restaurant after the evening service. We ate and chatted until around eight-thirty. When we arrived home, the boys were in bed, but not asleep; so we all talked for awhile. Around ten o'clock an idea for a new sermon series just seemed to pop into my head. I sat down and worked until after midnight. Now this is not my normal routine, after preaching three times in the morning and once in the evening. But I took advantage of my creative urge and experienced a very enjoyable study-planning session.

A fifth time-saver is to *always carry an idea sheet with you*. I use a clipboard. Some people carry a large yellow-lined tablet, others a small notebook. But whatever you choose, carry it faithfully. Then during those idle moments you will be able to jot down ideas, schedule your time, balance your budget, etc.

Here is a final essential for time management: prayer.

Prayer

I have personally found prayer to be a very effective tool in my own stewardship of time. I pray either (1) that the Lord will give me guidance in using my time most effectively and efficiently, or (2) that when my schedule seems impossible to keep, He will either change my schedule or increase my efficiency.

God has been very faithful in answering such prayers. Sometimes when I'm under the pressure of a full schedule, an appointment will be canceled, giving me a breather. Other times the Lord has seen fit to grant me a special measure of concentration so that I can accomplish twice the amount of work I normally could in the same amount of time. God is no respecter of persons. What He has done for me He will do for you.

You are responsible to use God's time in the most efficient and effective way you know. "Therefore be careful how you walk, not as unwise men, but as wise, *making the most of your time*, because the days are evil" (Eph. 5:15,16, italics mine).

12

You Can Overcome Temptation

Satan is the greatest force of evil on this earth. He is your enemy. He will do everything in his power to lower your resistance to temptation.

His allies include an immense host of demonic spirits, the anti-God world system, and the self-centered old nature. His arsenal of specific temptations includes overeating, abuse of alcoholic beverages, overspending, worry, pride, sexual immorality, an uncontrolled tongue, peer pressure, and the mismanagement of time.

Whatever your particular character traits or spiritual maturity, the devil has at least one tailor-made temptation for you. You may be a strong-willed individual. Don't be surprised if Satan defeats you with pride and an uncontrolled tongue. Or perhaps you are weak-willed. If so, he might tempt you with delicious delicacies, several excellent bargains you "can't" resist, alcoholic beverages, or peer pressure. Or suppose you are not too well organized. The devil may encourage you to waste time or to worry because you have so much to do. And whatever your traits or maturity, Satan will constantly suggest an alternative to God's moral principles.

The forces against you are powerful, and if you spend time thinking about them you will probably feel over-whelmed. You may conclude, "Wow, the pressure is too great. There's no way I can experience victory over temptation!" Satan would love for you to buy that philosophy. But it just isn't true.

The fact is victory already belongs to you. True, you should never underestimate your enemy, but don't compound the problem by underestimating your Ally.

God never expects you to do anything for which He has not equipped you. He expects you to resist temptation because He has provided you with a defense against each one of Satan's agents.

SATAN'S AGENT	GOD'S COUNTERAGENT
(1) Satan and his demonic world	(1) The Holy Spirit and the Holy Scriptures
(2) Satan working through the world system	(2) The Holy Spirit working through the church
(3) Satan working through the old nature	(3) The Holy Spirit working through the new nature

THE HOLY SPIRIT AND THE HOLY SCRIPTURES

Jesus resisted temptation by subjecting Himself to *the Spirit's power* rather than by using His own divine nature (Luke 4:1,2;13,14). In fact, His ministry was performed under the Spirit's power. The Jews accused Jesus of casting out demons by the power of Beelzebub, prince of the demons, but Jesus replied, "If Satan drives out Satan, he is divided against himself. How then can his kingdom stand? And if I drive out demons by Beelzebub, by whom do your people drive them out? So then, they will be your judges. But if I drive out demons by *the Spirit of God*, then the kingdom of God has come upon you" (Matt. 12:26–28, NIV, italics mine).

Concerning Jesus' ministering under the Spirit's influence rather than His own, Dr. John F. Walvoord wrote, "The incarnation and the self-limitation which this involved did not strip Christ of a single attribute; it only denied their independent use where this would conflict with his purpose to live among men as a man."*

If Jesus had resisted Satan by using His own divine strength, we could excuse ourselves from resisting temptation. We could reason, "Jesus withstood temptation because He was God. Since I'm not God, I certainly can't expect spiritual victory." But whenever Jesus faced Satan and his demons, He relied on the power of the Holy Spirit to defeat them.

God knows you need a power greater than yourself to withstand Satan, so He has provided Himself living in you. "Greater is He who is in you than he who is in the world" (1 John 4:4).

The apostle Paul revealed how God equips believers to face Satan and his demons. He first speaks about the Christian's *defensive* weapons—"The . . . strong belt of truth and the breastplate of God's approval. Wear shoes that speed you on as you preach the Good News of peace with God. In every battle you will need faith as your shield

*Walvoord, *The Holy Spirit* (Grand Rapids, Mich.: Zondervan, 1958), n.p.

to stop the fiery arrows aimed at you by Satan. And you will need the helmet of salvation . . ." Then he adds the one *offensive* weapon—"and the sword of the Spirit— which is the Word of God" (Eph. 6:14-17, TLB).

God's Word is a powerful weapon, but in order for that weapon to be effective in your encounter with Satan and his demons there are two basic requirements: (1) familiarity with the weapon, and (2) using the weapon in the power of the Spirit.

Be familiar with your weapon. When a soldier goes into basic training he is given a rifle. That weapon becomes his closest companion. He eats and sleeps with it. He must be able to take it apart and put it together again blindfolded. You are a solider of Jesus Christ (see 2 Tim. 23:3,4). Therefore you must be familiar with Scripture. Learn all you can through the instruction of others and from your own private reading and meditation.

Read so that you become familiar with both the Old and New Testaments. Take time to memorize God's promises and claim them for yourself. Develop an understanding of the principles that lead to spiritual prosperity. Learn how practical the Bible is for life situations such as loneliness, anger, frustration, moral temptations, fear, wrong attitudes, and effective husband-wife relationships.

Then when Satan confronts you with a specific temptation, *use God's Word in the power of the Holy Spirit*. For instance, let's say you have an opportunity to sell your car and you know your car uses a lot of oil. The prospective buyer asks you, "How is it on oil?" Immediately you face a decision. Should I (1) tell an outright lie? (2) play down the problem? (3) evade the question by pointing out the car's great gas mileage?

If you tell the buyer how badly the car uses oil, you may

have to sell the car for $150 to $200 less. You know what you ought to do, but you also need the money. Because you are familiar with God's Word, the Holy Spirit brings three passages to your mind. "Keep your lives free from the love of money and be content with what you have, because God has said, 'Never will I leave you; never will I forsake you' " (Heb. 13:5, NIV). "In everything do to others what you would have them do to you, for this sums up the Law and the Prophets" (Matt. 7:12, NIV). "You shall not bear false witness against your neighbor" (Exod. 20:16).

Now there is no question about what is right or wrong. You can't hedge by convincing yourself "everybody else does it." God's Word has clearly defined what you must do. So you accept God's verdict on honesty, answer the buyer's question directly, and maybe lose some money. In the process you have maintained a clear conscience, honored the Lord, and defeated the father of lies (see John 8:44).

I had the opportunity to put this very challenge into effect when I sold our 1964 Oldsmobile station wagon a few years ago. I told the buyer the car was a gas hog, used oil, and had a broken back window. The only benefits it offered were its size for carrying extras and a set of new but cheap tires. I thought he would offer $100 to $150. Instead he offered $250. I told him I would be pleased to accept this offer, but to make sure he had heard me I again listed the problems of the car. Since he was a mechanic, the problems didn't bother him. He just wanted cheap transportation, and his offer stood. I accepted with a clear conscience.

James summarizes how to face Satan and his demonic agents when he tempts you with pride. Again, the principles are to know what the Bible says and use it in God's power. "Or do you think that the Scripture speaks to no purpose: 'He jealously desires the spirit which He has made to dwell in us'? But He gives a greater grace. Therefore it says, 'God is opposed to the proud, but gives grace to the humble.' Submit therefore to God. Resist the devil and he will flee from you" (James 4:5-7).

Satan and his demonic world can be defeated by God's counteragents, the Holy Spirit and the Scriptures. But how can you deal with Satan when he uses the world system to tempt you?

THE HOLY SPIRIT WORKING
THROUGH THE CHURCH

What do the church and the world have in common? At first glance you might conclude they have very little in common. And yet, they are designed to fulfill similar functions.

The world system offers its clubs, organizations, and places of entertainment. It wants you to join in its life-style and adopt the "do your own thing" philosophy of life. The friendships are often shallow and the smiles at times are like paint on a clown's face. Within the world system there is emptiness and alienation from God. "You adulterous people, don't you know that friendship with the world is hatred toward God? Anyone who chooses to be a friend of the world becomes an enemy of God" (James 4:4, NIV).

Concerning social life in the world system Peter said, "For you have spent enough time in the past doing what pagans choose to do—living in debauchery, lust, drunkenness, orgies, carousing, and detestable idolatry. They think it strange that you do not plunge with them into the same flood of dissipation, and they heap abuse on you" (1 Pet. 4:3,4, NIV)

"But if I can't belong to the world, to what group can I belong? How else can I feel accepted or needed?" The Lord offers you His church.

The church is a fellowship for you. It needs you (1 Cor. 12:14-20) and you need it (1 Cor. 12:21-24). The church is designed primarily to meet man's spiritual needs (Eph. 4:11-16). But it is also responsible for physical needs (1 Tim. 5:3-15; 2 Cor. 8:1-7; 9:12-15), emotional needs (1 Cor. 12:15,26), and fellowship (Gal. 2:9,10).

When the church functions the way God designed it and when you avail yourself to get involved, there is little need to become entangled in the world system. The Holy Spirit will meet your needs through the body of Christ. You will belong. You will have a ministry. You will experience the fulfillment God has planned for you.

True, all churches don't function to meet needs. Some seem to have lost their purpose. But others are creatively fulfilling the purpose for which God designed them.

Wherever needs have existed, the church has been on the scene. Think for a moment. Who started the first universities of this country? Who has established hospitals and care for the elderly around the world? Who is on the scene immediately after a flood, tornado, hurricane, fire, or earthquake? The church at large has a history of healing the sick, feeding the hungry, educating the ignorant, caring for the widows, orphans, and elderly, offering eternal life to the lost, and providing biblical teaching for growing Christians.

The world may promise a lot, but it delivers little. However, when the Holy Spirit is allowed to work through the church, he will meet both temporal and eternal needs. Now consider the third counteragent—your new inner self.

THE HOLY SPIRIT AND YOUR NEW
INNER SELF

You possess a sinful nature that can be traced back to Adam (Rom. 5:12). When you sin, that sin originates from within, not from external causes. Jesus said, "Don't you see that whatever enters the mouth goes into the stomach and then out of the body? But the things that come out of the mouth come from the heart, and these make a man 'unclean'. For out of the heart come evil thoughts, murder, adultery, sexual immorality, theft, false testimony, slander" (Matt. 15:17–19, NIV).

But when you receive Jesus Christ into your life, God gives you a new capacity or nature. Paul described the qualities of this new nature to the Colossian believers: "Therefore, as God's chosen people, holy and dearly loved, clothe yourselves with compassion, kindness, humility, gentleness and patience" (Col. 3:12, NIV). What a contrast between the old self and the new! The former leads you into sin while the latter paves the way for a spiritually productive life.

But the question remains, "How can I activate my new nature and disarm my old nature?" The answer is simple, You must not depend on your own strength but rely on the Holy Spirit. If the mere possession of a new nature kept us from sin, there would be no carnal Christians. But the fact that many Christians live defeated and spiritually unproductive lives is evidence enough that we need more than a new nature. We need an energy source to activate that nature.

The other day I was using a pocket calculator when suddenly it stopped working. No amount of shaking helped. The problem, I soon discovered, was a dead battery. The calculator had the same potential as before, but the power source had died. Had I not replaced the dead battery, that pocket calculator with all its potential would have remained useless.

Your new nature has the potential to successfully resist temptation, but it must be empowered by the Holy Spirit. How then can you connect the Spirit of God with your new nature? You connect to your power supply by faith. Just as you receive Jesus Christ by personally inviting Him into your life (an act of faith or believing, see John 1:12), so you can invite the Holy Spirit to control your life (an act of faith, see 1 John 5:14,15 and Eph. 5:18).

Let's look at this further. Faith is believing and acting upon a fact. If I want to fly to New York from San Francisco, I first check out which airlines fly that route. Then I buy my ticket, arrive at the airport about an hour before the plane leaves, board the plane, and fly to New York. Each of these acts is based upon my belief (faith) that the airline will do exactly what it promises to do. (Sometimes my faith has been overextended in such cases!) Likewise, when you live by faith you are believing that God will do exactly as He promises. Now see how this truth works concerning the Holy Spirit's ministry in your life.

I. THE FACT

"We have this assurance in approaching God, that *if we ask anything* according to his will, he hears us. And if we know that he hears us—whatever we

ask—we know that we have what we asked of him"
(1 John 5:14,15, NIV, italics mine).

II. GOD'S STATED WILL

"Do not get drunk on wine, which leads to
debauchery. Instead, *be filled with the Spirit*" (Eph.
5:18, NIV, italics mine). ("Keep on being filled" is
the literal translation.)

III. YOUR FAITH PUT INTO EFFECT

1. When sin has broken your fellowship with God

    "Lord, I confess that I've been running my
    life on my own terms. I now turn it over to
    You. I ask that Your Holy Spirit will take over
    my life ."

2. When you are still in fellowship with God

    "Lord, thank you that your Spirit has been
    controlling my life. This morning (after-
    noon, evening) I give Him permission to
    continue His ministry in me."

IV. THE RESULT

"So I say, live by the Spirit, and *you will not
gratify the desires of your sinful nature*. For the
sinful nature desires what is contrary to the
Spirit, and the Spirit what is contrary to the
sinful nature. They are in conflict with each
other, so that you do not do what you want"
(Gal. 5:16,17, NIV, italics mine).

God has done His part by supplying you with a new
potential to resist temptation (the new inner self) and the
power source to activate that nature (the Holy Spirit).

Your responsibility is to continuously act in faith on His promises and expect good results.

Satan confronts you every day. You cannot run away. You must stand and fight. And you can win because God has supplied you with superior forces.

To withstand Satan's demonic forces God has given you His Word.

To overcome Satan's world system, God provides His church.

To counteract Satan's work through your old inner self, God created a new nature. When God's Holy Spirit is allowed to use the Word, empower the church, and control the new inner self, victory is certain.

Therefore, adopt a new outlook on life. Put aside the thought that spiritual defeat is inevitable. Recognize instead that victory is certain. *You can overcome temptation!*

Recommended Reading

Chapter 1

Breese, Dave. *His Infernal Majesty*. Chicago: Moody Press, 1974.
Lindsell, Harold. *The World, the Flesh, and the Devil*. Grand Rapids, Mich.: Baker.
Unger, Merrill F. *Demons in the World Today*. Wheaton, Ill.: Tyndale House. 1972.
White, John Wesley. *The Devil: What the Scriptures Teach about Him*. Wheaton, Ill.: Tyndale House, 1977.

Chapter 2

Hunter, Frances. *God's Answer to Fat-Lose It*. Houston: Hunter Ministries, 1976.
Levitt, Zola. *How to Win at Losing*. Wheaton, Ill.: Tyndale House, 1975.
Rohrer, Virginia and Norman. *How to Eat Right and Feel Great*. Wheaton, Ill.: Tyndale House, 1977.
Shedd, Charlie W. *The Fat Is in Your Head*. Waco, Tex.: Word, 1972.

Chapter 3

Draper, James T. Jr., *Proverbs: The Secret of Beautiful Living*, chapter 12. Wheaton, Ill.: Tyndale House, 1977.

164

Dunn, Jerry G. *God Is for the Alcoholic*. Chicago: Moody Press, 1967.
Palmer, Bernard. *My Son, My Son*. Chicago: Moody Press, 1970.
Soergel, Mary. *Sing a Gentle Breeze*. Wheaton, Ill.: Tyndale House, 1977.

Chapter 4

Bowman, George. *How to Succeed with Your Money*. Chicago: Moody Press, 1960.
Fooshee, George Jr. *You Can Be Financially Free*. Old Tappan, N.J.: Revell, 1976.
Otis, George. *God, Money and You*. Van Nuys, Calif.: Bible Voice.
Page, Carole G. *Let Not Money Put Asunder What God Has Joined Together*. Denver, Accent.

Chapter 5

Bisagno, John. *The Power of Postive Praying*. Grand Rapids, Mich.: Zondervan, 1965.
Carothers, R. Merlin. *Prison to Praise*. Plainfield, N.J.: Logos, 1970.
Gutzke, Manford G. *Plain Talk on Prayer*. Grand Rapids, Mich.: Baker, 1973.
Rinker, Rosalind. *Prayer: Conversing with God*. Grand Rapids, Mich.: Zondervan.

Chapter 6

Draper, James T. Jr. *Proverbs: The Secret of Beautiful Living*, chapter 5. Wheaton, Ill.: Tyndale House, 1977.
Morris, Paul D. *Love Therapy*, chapter 9, Wheaton, Ill.: Tyndale House, 1975.

Chapter 7

Banowsky, William S. *It's a Playboy World*. Old Tappan, N.J.: Revell, 1969.
Benson, Dan. *The Total Man*, chapters 18-20. Wheaton, Ill.: Tyndale house, 1977.
Miles, Herbert J. *Sexual Happiness in Marriage*. Grand Rapids, Mich.: Zondervan, 1967.
Trobisch, Walter. *Love Is a Feeling to Be Learned*. Downers Grove, Ill.: Inter-Varsity Press, 1968.

Chapter 8

Draper, James T. Jr. *Proverbs: The Secret of Beautiful Living*, chapter 14. Wheaton, Ill.: Tyndale House, 1977.

Chapter 9

Ausgburger, David. *Be All You Can Be*. Carol Stream, Ill.: Creation House.

Gangel, Kenneth O. *Leadership for Church Education*. Chicago: Moody Press, 1970.

Sanders, J. Oswald. *Spiritual Leadership*. Chicago: Moody Press, 1974.

Chapter 10

Bland, Glenn. *Success: The Glenn Bland Method*. Wheaton, Ill.: Tyndale House, 1975.

Engstrom, Ted W. and MacKenzie, Alex. *Managing Your Time*. Grand Rapids, Mich.: Zondervan, 1968.

Chapter 11

Adams, Lane. *How Come It's Taking Me So Long to Get Better?* Wheaton, Ill.: Tyndale House, 1975.

Augsburger, David. *So What? Everybody's Doing it*. Chicago: Moody Press, 1969.

Schaeffer, Francis. *True Spirituality*. Wheaton, Ill.: Tyndale House, 1971.

Smith, Hannah W. *The Christian's Secret of a Happy Life*. Old Tappan, N.J.: Revell, 1968.

About the Author

Rick Yohn is pastor of The Evangelical Free Church of Fresno, California. He is the author of ten books and has been named to *Who's Who in Religion, Who's Who in the West,* and *Who's Who in America.* He received his bachelor's degree from Philadelphia College of Bible, his master's degree from Dallas Theological Seminary, and his doctorate from Talbot Theological Seminary in LaMirada, California. Both his writing and speaking are known for their biblical, easy to understand, practical style.